Common Law Courts and Sheriffs: Restoring the Authority of the People

Roger Davies

Published by TWON Publications, 2025.

COMMON LAW COURTS AND SHERIFFS: RESTORING THE AUTHORITY OF THE PEOPLE

First edition. November 30, 2025.

ISBN: 979-8231379279

Written by Roger Davies.

Table of Contents

INTRODUCTION 1

THE ORIGIN OF THE PEOPLE'S AUTHORITY 6

WHY STATUTORY COURTS LOST THEIR LEGITIMACY 15

THE RISE OF THE STRAWMAN IN MODERN COURTS 24

WHAT A COMMON LAW COURT IS 33

HOW A COMMON LAW COURT IS FORMED 42

THE ROLE OF A COMMON LAW SHERIFF 50

ELECTING A COMMON LAW SHERIFF 59

JURISDICTION AND THE POWER OF CONSENT 67

RUNNING HEARINGS IN A COMMON LAW COURT 75

COMMON LAW ENFORCEMENT 84

LIMITATIONS OF COMMON LAW COURTS 93

BUILDING A COMMUNITY COURT SYSTEM 102

THE COURT OF THE LIVING 111

Dedication

To the men and women who refuse silence.To those who stand in honour when others step back.To every soul who knows that authority comes from the living, not from institutions.This book is for you.

Epigraph

True authority begins when the living speak and ends when they remain silent.A people who stand in honour cannot be ruled by assumption.

INTRODUCTION

Freedom belongs to the living. It does not come from governments. It does not come from statutes. It does not come from corporate offices hiding behind uniforms, robes, and policy. Freedom is a birthright that exists because you were born. Every man and every woman enters this world with natural authority. That authority is higher than any office that claims power. It is higher than any statute printed on paper. It is higher than any institution that pretends to speak for the people.

For generations the truth of that authority has been buried. The system has taught people to believe that only government can give permission, resolve disputes, or maintain peace. The system has trained people to look down rather than stand tall, to ask permission rather than act with honour. The system has convinced millions that they are subjects of policy rather than living men and women with natural rights.

Common law courts and common law sheriffs expose that deception. They bring the authority of the people back to the surface. They remind every man and woman that law does not come from an office. It comes from truth, honour, and consent. Common law is not complex. It is not wrapped in codes or controlled by hidden language. Common law rests on three simple duties. Do no harm. Cause no loss. Commit no fraud. Every living soul understands these duties without instruction.

A lawful system is built on these duties. Once harm, loss, or fraud is removed, peace exists in a community. A court is only needed when those duties are broken. A sheriff is only needed to protect the peace when those duties are threatened. That is the origin of authority. Not legislation. Not policy. Not codes written by corporations. Authority comes from the people. It always has. The system fears this truth because it exposes the weakness of every statutory court in the land.

A statutory court depends on compliance. It depends on names written in capital letters. It depends on roles like resident, defendant, and citizen. It depends on silence. Consent is assumed because most people do not know how to challenge it. They walk into courtrooms believing that the judge outranks them. They speak without understanding that their own words can bind them into a commercial process. They answer to a name on paper rather than standing as a living soul. They step into the trap without realising that the trap was set centuries ago.

Common law courts break that pattern. They strip away every illusion. They recognise only the living. They reject the corporate version of the man or woman. They show that the ordinary person holds more authority than any office. They operate with honour, open truth, and community recognition. Their power does not come from force. Their power comes from consent and standing. When a group of men and women form a court under common law, they act with the natural authority that existed long before governments.

Common law sheriffs serve the same purpose. A sheriff under common law is not an employee of the state. A sheriff is not a policy enforcer. A sheriff is not controlled by statutory codes. A sheriff is chosen by the people to defend natural rights, protect the weak, stand against unlawful interference, and ensure peace. This role is older than any police force. It existed when communities lived by honour and did not rely on bureaucracy. A sheriff was known and trusted. A sheriff acted for the people and had no master except the truth.

Communities today feel the absence of that authority. They see police enforcing policy rather than protecting peace. They see councils issuing demands rather than serving the people. They see courts that trade in paperwork rather than justice. They see officials who claim power but cannot show a lawful source for it. They see a world run by corporations pretending to be governments. They see harm done in the name of policy. They see loss caused by taxation. They see fraud hidden behind procedure. They see a system that calls itself lawful while ignoring the simple duties of natural law.

The return of common law courts and sheriffs is a response to this loss of truth. When people gather to form a court, they are not rebelling. They are restoring. They are returning to the root of authority. They are removing the illusion that law belongs to offices. They are reclaiming responsibility for justice. They are standing in honour rather than fear.

A common law court is simple. It does not require robes. It does not require titles. It does not require buildings with crests and flags. It requires only this. Living men and women standing together and agreeing to hear a matter with truth and fairness. They choose a foreman. They listen to evidence. They decide based on honour. They record their judgment. This process is lawful because it is rooted in natural authority. It is lawful because consent is present. It is lawful because no corporate fiction is involved.

A common law sheriff is simple. He is elected by the people. He accepts an oath to protect life, property, and peace. He does not enforce statutes. He enforces honour. He responds to harm, not policy. He protects the vulnerable. He serves notices when a community decision is made. He stands against trespass by corporations acting without consent. The authority of a sheriff comes from the living, not the state. That is why the system fears this role. It cannot control a sheriff chosen by the people.

For many, the idea of creating a common law court feels new. In truth it is the oldest form of justice. Communities solved disputes long before governments existed. Men sat together around fires, in halls, in fields, and in homes. They resolved matters by agreement. They listened to those who had been harmed. They required restitution when needed. They acted as caretakers of peace, not rulers. The first courts were gatherings of the people. The first sheriffs were chosen by the people. Every modern system came later and replaced truth with procedure.

This book is written to restore that truth. It is written for every man and woman who senses that something is wrong but cannot put words to it. It is written for those who know that statutory courts feel like theatres. It is written for those who see police acting as revenue agents rather than guardians. It is written for those who have faced harm from councils and agencies who claim authority that has never been proven. It is written for those who want to protect their families and communities with honour rather than fear.

Throughout this book you will see a clear thread. The people hold authority. Statutory bodies only claim authority. The difference between claiming and holding is consent. Once consent is withdrawn, the illusion fades. A community that stands together under common law becomes stronger than any office. Natural law outranks statute because natural law comes from life itself. Statute is only policy written by corporations.

You will learn how common law courts operate. You will learn how a community can form one. You will learn how to stand as a living man or woman in honour. You will learn how consent shapes jurisdiction. You will learn the duties of a common law sheriff. You will learn how elections work and why accountability matters. You will learn how to recognise harm, loss, and fraud when they appear in your community. You will learn how to support others when the system uses intimidation. You will learn how honour removes fear.

This book will give clarity to those who want to understand their natural standing. It will give strength to those who want to act. It will give structure to those who want to build community courts. It will give direction to those who want freedom without conflict. It will show that the path to lawful authority is peaceful, steady, and grounded in truth.

There is a shift happening. People across the country are questioning authority. They are rejecting commercial courts. They are exposing fraud. They are standing as living souls. They are teaching each other how consent works. They are recording their notices. They are forming assemblies. They are restoring peace without waiting for permission. They are realising that they do not need the state to give them rights. Rights do not come from the state. Rights come from life.

Common law courts and common law sheriffs are part of that awakening. They are not new. They are a return to the original order of things. They remind the people that they always had the power. They remind the people that authority lies with them by nature. Once this truth is remembered, nothing can remove it. Not paperwork. Not threats. Not policy. Not procedure. A living man who knows his authority cannot be bound by a fiction. A community that stands in honour cannot be controlled by fear.

This book is a guide for those who are ready to take that stand. It is written to bring clarity, structure, and confidence. It is written to remind you of what you already know. Law belongs to the living. Authority belongs to the people. Peace belongs to the community. The time has come to restore these truths. The time has come to stand together. The time has come to return to common law.

THE ORIGIN OF THE PEOPLE'S AUTHORITY

Authority begins with the living. It starts the moment a man takes his first breath. It starts the moment a woman opens her eyes to the world. No office creates this authority. No institution grants it. No signature or document gives it form. It belongs to the living by nature. It is not something learned, earned, or awarded. It is part of life itself. This truth shaped the earliest communities long before governments existed and long before corporate systems began claiming control over the people.

Natural authority is simple. A man understands harm without reading a statute. A woman recognises loss without being taught. Children know that truth matters and that deception causes damage. These principles do not come from councils, courts, or parliaments. They come from nature. They come from conscience. Every living soul is born with the internal ability to understand basic fairness. It is the foundation that all genuine law rests upon.

In ancient communities, authority flowed from the people. Villages did not rely on distant rulers to tell them how to solve disputes. They relied on truth, dialogue, and honour. When harm occurred, the community acted. When loss appeared, the people restored balance. When deception was uncovered, the group held the wrongdoer accountable. There were no layers of bureaucracy. No controlled police forces. No judges working behind closed doors. Justice was direct, open, and honest. It belonged to the living.

These early forms of justice created the first true courts. The people gathered in open spaces. They listened to those affected. They weighed truth against evidence. They reached decisions through agreement, not intimidation. Respect held the process together. The authority of the court came from the people, not from rulers or officials. This is why these gatherings are recognised as the true roots of common law. They functioned with clarity because the people understood their natural standing.

Natural authority is grounded in responsibility. A man who harms another must put it right. A woman who causes loss must restore it. A person who acts in dishonour must answer for that act. Responsibility and authority rise together. They cannot be separated. When the people hold authority, they also hold responsibility. When institutions take authority, responsibility weakens and the people become dependent. That dependence is what allowed governments and corporations to grow beyond their natural limits.

Authority began to shift when institutions positioned themselves between the people and their own natural rights. Rulers claimed divine authority. Courts claimed superior knowledge. Governments claimed power through documents, seals, and procedures. Step by step, these institutions created distance between themselves and the people. They used symbols to elevate their status. They used uniforms to create fear. They used complex language to confuse the population. As this happened, the people slowly stopped seeing themselves as the source of law.

This change did not occur in a single moment. It unfolded over centuries. Each generation handed a little more authority to institutions. Each generation allowed procedures to replace honour. Each generation tolerated systems that felt unnatural because they believed the institutions knew better. Over time, the people forgot how to govern themselves. They forgot how simple justice was before institutions complicated it. They forgot that law flows from the living, not from offices.

Natural authority remained, even during those times. It cannot die. It cannot be removed. It cannot be taken by any system. It only becomes hidden beneath layers of conditioning. That is why, in every era, men and women have stood up and reminded others of their natural rights. They saw the imbalance. They felt the distortion. They recognised that institutions had exceeded their rightful place. These men and women spoke truth because truth does not require permission. Truth stands on its own.

The modern world suffers from the same imbalance. Governments treat statutes as if they were higher than life. Courts treat procedures as if they were more important than truth. Police forces act as if policy enforcement is justice. Councils behave like corporate bodies collecting revenue rather than supporting communities. The people sense the imbalance. They feel it when decisions are made without their consent. They feel it when they are treated as legal fictions rather than living souls. They feel it when institutions ignore harm, loss, or fraud yet push forward with demands, penalties, and notices.

This loss of natural order happens because the people forget the origin of their authority. Institutions only hold power when the people believe they do. Once belief fades, natural authority resurfaces. A living man does not bow to a document that contradicts truth. A living woman does not surrender her voice to a policy that exists only to control. A community that remembers its authority does not obey institutions that have stepped outside honour.

Natural authority returns through recognition, not rebellion. It does not need force. It does not need anger. It only needs clarity. When the people recognise they are the true source of law, the system that relies on their silence becomes weak. That is why modern institutions work so hard to create confusion. Confusion is their strongest tool. They use complex wording to hide simple truths. They use layered procedures to distract people from the foundation of law. They use titles to create psychological distance between officials and the public. They use paperwork to replace honour with bureaucracy.

The legal fiction is a perfect example of this confusion. A name written in capital letters on a document is treated as if it were the living soul. Institutions interact with the fiction, not the man. They address the fiction as the responsible party. They issue demands to the fiction. They create obligations for the fiction. But a fiction cannot think, speak, act, or breathe. Only a living man or woman can do that. The fiction is a tool created by institutions. It only gains power when the living respond to it without asserting their natural standing.

This focus on the legal fiction allowed institutions to extend their reach into daily life. Instead of dealing with the living, they deal with the construct they created. The people unknowingly act as surety for that construct. Procedures are built around the fiction. Statutes are written for the fiction. Penalties are issued against the fiction. Courts operate as commercial venues dealing with the fiction. When a man or woman answers as the fiction, consent is assumed. Jurisdiction is assumed. Authority is assumed. The living step into the system because they do not realise they have a choice.

Natural authority is the antidote to this structure. A living soul who knows their standing cannot be forced into acting as a fiction. They speak in their own voice. They stand in truth. They refuse roles that are applied without consent. They question every claim made by institutions. They demand proof of authority. They insist on honour. These actions are not extreme. They are natural. They are simple. They are the way law worked for thousands of years before institutions complicated it.

Communities are beginning to recognise this again. People are forming assemblies. They are learning the principles of common law. They are discovering how natural authority works. They are questioning statutory claims. They are reminding each other that law belongs to the living. This awakening is not disruptive. It is restorative. It restores dignity, clarity, and honesty. It removes fear from the process of justice. It brings people back to their proper place as the foundation of all law.

This is the true origin of authority. It is not found in government buildings. It is not found in documents sealed with emblems. It is not found in corporate registers. It is found within the living. Every man and woman carries natural authority from birth. It cannot be handed away unless the individual forgets they possess it. Once remembered, it rises again with strength, clarity, and honour.

Natural authority is lived, not theorised. You see it in daily interactions whenever two people resolve a disagreement through honest conversation. You see it when a man apologises for causing harm and restores what was lost. You see it when a woman steps forward to protect someone who has been mistreated. These actions happen without government instruction. They happen without legal training. They happen because humans understand fairness instinctively. Fairness is a natural force that guides behaviour and restores balance. It is older than every statute on earth.

This natural force shaped the earliest communities. Hierarchies were simple because they relied on trust, not power. Elders were respected for wisdom, not authority. Sheriffs were chosen for honour, not control. Courts were gatherings, not institutions. Justice was a community duty, not a commercial process. There was no need for distant structures to interpret right and wrong. People understood these principles because the principles lived within them.

As societies grew, their structures changed. Rulers wanted central control. Officials wanted influence. Institutions wanted permanence. These desires led to the creation of formal systems. Those systems grew in size and complexity. Over time they pushed natural authority to the background. People began to believe they could not act lawfully without permission. They believed they needed officials to solve their disputes. They believed the role of the living soul was small, while the role of the institution was large.

This shift created a world where the people forgot they were the source of all authority. They forgot that rulers once asked permission from communities, not the other way around. They forgot that law was originally spoken, lived, and understood, not written, coded, and enforced. They forgot that justice belonged to them. This forgetting allowed institutions to expand beyond their rightful limits. It allowed courts to become revenue centres. It allowed governments to treat statutes as if they were superior to natural law. It allowed corporations to guide policy. All of this happened because the people forgot their natural standing.

Yet even during periods of heavy institutional control, the truth remained in the background. There were always individuals who recognised that the power claimed by institutions depended entirely on belief. They saw that the living held the true authority. They saw that no statute could override conscience. They saw that harm, loss, and fraud were still the only genuine violations, no matter what the codes and regulations said. They understood that institutions only operated through presumed consent. They knew the system could only function if the people remained silent.

Silence creates jurisdiction. It allows institutions to treat the living as legal fictions without resistance. Once a man responds to the fiction, the system considers him bound. Once a woman accepts the role written on a document, the institution assumes she has stepped into its jurisdiction. This is why so much of the system's power rests on paperwork. Paperwork is the bridge between the fiction and the living. When the living step onto that bridge without asserting their standing, the system takes control.

Natural authority dissolves that bridge. A living soul who speaks in their own right stands outside the fiction. They require institutions to prove their claims. They insist on honour. They question jurisdiction. They hold their ground calmly. These actions expose the weakness of systems that depend on assumption. They reveal that much of modern law functions as commercial procedure rather than genuine justice. They remind institutions that their authority is borrowed, not inherent.

The system hides this by using complexity. Complexity is a tool of control. When law becomes difficult to understand, people assume officials are necessary. They assume only experts can interpret the rules. They assume authority lies with those who understand the complex language. This belief keeps people dependent. It prevents them from remembering how simple law truly is. When people forget simplicity, they forget natural authority. When they forget natural authority, institutions expand.

The truth remains unchanged. Law is simple. The duties are clear. Harm, loss, and fraud create disputes. Everything else is procedure. A statute that does not address harm, loss, or fraud is not law. It is policy. A regulation that governs behaviour without addressing natural principles is not law. It is instruction. Institutions enforce these instructions as if they were law, but they only succeed when the people accept them without question.

Natural authority empowers the living to question everything. It reminds a man that he is not bound by corporate policy. It reminds a woman that she is not required to surrender her voice. It reminds a community that its collective power is greater than any institution acting without consent. These reminders weaken the hold of systems built on silence. They bring clarity to the people. They strengthen the foundation of honour. They restore the balance that existed long before statutory control.

When communities reconnect with natural authority, something powerful happens. Fear dissolves. The people stop seeing institutions as superior. They stop believing that officials hold some special power. They stop thinking they must comply with rules that do not align with natural law. They begin to stand with confidence. They begin to support each other. They begin to challenge unlawful claims. This collective change shifts the balance away from centralised control and back toward the people.

Natural authority brings responsibility along with strength. When the people reclaim authority, they must also uphold honour. They must resolve their own disputes. They must treat each other with fairness. They must act openly and truthfully. Authority without honour becomes abuse. Honour without authority becomes silence. The two must remain together for common law to function. This is why common law courts and sheriffs rely on community recognition. They rely on people acting responsibly.

Institutions fear communities that uphold natural authority because such communities cannot be controlled easily. They cannot be manipulated through paperwork. They cannot be intimidated by titles. They cannot be swayed by threats. Their strength comes from within. Their authority comes from life. Institutions that rely on commercial structures cannot compete with natural law. Natural law is older, purer, and rooted in truth.

This is the foundation upon which common law courts stand. They arise from the people, not from the state. Their legitimacy comes from living recognition. Their process is grounded in fairness, not procedure. Their decisions are based on truth, not policy. They serve the living, not the fiction. This structure is lawful because it reflects natural authority. A community acting in honour holds the highest form of law. The system knows this, even if it pretends otherwise.

The same foundation supports the role of the common law sheriff. A sheriff chosen by the people acts with natural authority. He protects peace because the people entrusted him with that duty. He enforces natural principles because he serves the living. He does not answer to institutions that ignore honour. His oath is to truth, not to corporate bodies. His authority rises from the people, flows through the people, and remains accountable to the people. This is why his role is feared by statutory systems. They cannot claim control over him.

Natural authority therefore forms the base of every lawful action a community takes. It cannot be replaced by statutes. It cannot be redefined by courts. It cannot be rewritten by government departments. It exists because the living exist. Institutions can only borrow authority through consent. When consent is not given, their claims fall apart. This is the core truth that modern systems attempt to conceal beneath layers of procedure.

The people are beginning to remember this truth. As they do, they reclaim the strength that was always theirs. They speak more clearly. They stand more firmly. They see through intimidation. They recognise the difference between law and policy. They question everything that does not align with natural principles. Each act of recognition restores authority to the correct source. When enough people remember, the natural order returns.

Authority belongs to the living. It always has. It always will. It does not start in government. It starts in life. It does not begin with institutions. It begins with truth. It does not rise from statutes. It rises from conscience. Every man and every woman carries it. Every community can use it. Nothing can remove it, only conceal it. Once remembered, it becomes unshakeable.

WHY STATUTORY COURTS LOST THEIR LEGITIMACY

Statutory courts present themselves as the highest authority in the land. They speak through robes, elevated benches, formal language, and strict procedure. They behave as if their power is absolute. They expect the people to believe that their rulings stand above all other forms of law. Yet when you examine how these courts operate, you see a system built on assumptions, not truth. You see a process held together by consent, not natural authority. You see a structure that has drifted far away from the original principles of law.

A statutory court does not begin with the living. It begins with the legal fiction. Every case is framed around a name written on paper. That name is treated as the party to the action. It is the entity brought before the court. It is the entity judged. It is the entity fined. Yet this name is not alive. It cannot speak, think, or act. It exists only in documents held by institutions. The statutory system relies on this fiction because it allows the court to treat law as commercial procedure rather than natural justice.

When the living man or woman walks into the courtroom without asserting their standing, the system assumes they are acting as the fiction. Once this assumption is made, the court believes it holds authority over them. This authority is not based on natural law. It is based on contract. The moment the living responds in the role of the fiction, the court assumes consent. Consent creates jurisdiction. Jurisdiction allows the court to proceed as if the individual has agreed to be bound by statutory rules.

This process is rarely explained to the public. People are taught that courts have automatic authority. They believe the judge's position gives him power over their lives. They think the building itself carries lawful force. They assume the process is grounded in justice. They are never told that the entire structure depends on one silent expectation. The expectation is that the living will not challenge their status. That expectation keeps the statutory court functioning.

True law does not hide behind expectation. True law is open and direct. Early courts in common law tradition operated openly. The people knew the process. They understood the rules. They knew who held authority because they were the authority. Those courts existed to resolve harm, loss, and fraud. They did not exist to enforce policy. They did not generate revenue. They did not act in service of institutions. They acted in service of truth.

Statutory courts moved away from this purpose. They became instruments for enforcing codes and regulations that do not reflect natural law. They treat breaches of policy as if they were crimes. They focus on procedure rather than harm. They push forward with cases even when no living soul has suffered loss. They issue fines for acts that cause no injury. They punish behaviour that offends a regulation rather than a principle. These actions break the foundation of law. A court that ignores natural principles loses legitimacy.

The shift from natural justice to statutory enforcement happened gradually. Governments expanded their power by writing codes that covered every aspect of life. Councils created regulations to increase control. Agencies produced rules that governed behaviour. Each code and regulation was framed as law, yet none originated from natural principles. They were corporate instructions dressed as legislation. Statutory courts became the tool used to enforce them.

These courts operate as administrative venues. They manage cases like transactions. They rely on paperwork to determine outcomes. They accept documents as truth without questioning the intent behind them. They treat the legal fiction as the accountable party and expect the living to act as surety. The entire system functions like a commercial process, not a court of law. This is why statutory courts feel cold, mechanical, and disconnected from justice. They are not designed to uphold honour. They are designed to enforce policy.

Another sign of lost legitimacy is the role of the judge. In statutory courts the judge is not an impartial servant of the people. He is an administrator of statutory rules. His duty is to uphold the code, not natural law. He cannot act outside the legislation that created his office. This restriction prevents him from applying natural justice even when he recognises the truth. The people expect judges to act with fairness, but fairness is not the foundation of his authority. His authority comes from statute, and statute serves institutions, not individuals.

A judge enforces the commercial rules of the system. He manages appearances, submissions, and documents. He interprets legislation as instructed. He treats silence as consent. He treats participation as acceptance of jurisdiction. The public sees the robe and believes it represents wisdom. In reality the robe represents an office bound to statutory procedure. This is why judges often avoid addressing harm or loss directly. Their role is to apply statutory rules, not natural principles.

For a system to remain legitimate it must align with truth. When a system drifts from truth, it becomes hollow. That is what happened to statutory courts. They continue to operate because the people believe they must comply. They continue to demand obedience because the people assume they are lawful. They continue to enforce policy because the people have forgotten the difference between law and instruction. The system survives through belief, not legitimacy.

Institutions rely on this belief. They use symbols to reinforce it. Crests placed above the judge's bench. Flags positioned behind the court. Raised platforms that elevate officials above the public. These symbols are intended to create psychological authority. They imply superiority. They imply distance. They imply control. Yet symbols carry no lawful weight. Authority is not created through decoration. Authority is created through consent. Without consent, symbols become meaningless.

The people also give away authority through fear. Many walk into statutory courts feeling intimidated. They assume the judge holds absolute power. They believe they cannot challenge anything. They follow instructions without understanding them. This fear strengthens the illusion. A system that depends on fear cannot be legitimate. A lawful system earns trust. It does not demand submission. It does not threaten silence. It does not punish those who ask for clarity.

Another sign of lost legitimacy is the absence of accountability. Statutory courts are protected from challenge. Their officials are shielded by layers of procedure. Their decisions are enforced by police who act as policy officers, not peace officers. These protections create a structure where officials hold power without facing direct responsibility. Natural law does not allow this. In a common law community, authority and accountability rise together. A sheriff who abuses authority loses his position. A court that acts without honour loses its standing. The statutory system avoids accountability by hiding behind its own rules.

The loss of legitimacy becomes clear when you observe how statutory courts treat the people. They speak to the living as if they were subjects. They treat the legal fiction as if it were a real person. They refuse to recognise natural standing. They intimidate those who question jurisdiction. They avoid any discussion about consent. They respond to simple questions with complex answers designed to confuse. These behaviours reveal a system clinging to authority rather than serving the people.

Natural authority exposes these cracks. When a man stands confidently as the living soul, the statutory court struggles to maintain its script. When a woman speaks without accepting the role of the fiction, the court loses its assumed authority. When a community withdraws consent, institutions cannot function. This is why statutory courts avoid acknowledging natural law. They know it outranks statute. They know it empowers the people. They know it reveals the limits of their jurisdiction.

The people are beginning to see through the illusion. They are recognising that statutory courts serve the system, not the public. They see fines issued without harm. They see penalties enforced without loss. They see cases dismissed when people assert their standing. They see the power of consent. They see that natural authority remains superior to statutory procedure. As this recognition grows, the legitimacy of statutory courts continues to weaken.

A statutory court claims jurisdiction through paperwork, not through living authority. Every action they take begins with a document. A claim form. A charge sheet. A summons. A notice. A written allegation created by an institution, not by a living soul who has suffered harm or loss. This reliance on documents reveals the true nature of statutory courts. They do not operate on natural principles. They operate on administrative processing. They take written statements as if they were truth. They treat printed words as if they carry natural law. They elevate procedure above fairness.

This approach contradicts the original purpose of a court. The purpose of a court is to uncover truth. It is to examine facts. It is to repair harm. It is to restore balance. It is to hold people accountable when they act in dishonour. A statutory court rarely engages with these duties. Instead, it focuses on the mechanics of compliance. It demands correct forms. It requires specific phrasing. It expects the fiction to follow rules that the living never agreed to. This is not law. It is administration.

Administration is not illegitimate by itself. Organisations need administrative processes to function. Yet administration becomes illegitimate when it replaces justice. That is what has happened in statutory courts. They moved from serving the people to serving the system. They shifted their priority from fairness to revenue. They replaced harm with policy violations. They replaced loss with statutory fees. They replaced fraud with regulatory breaches. These replacements distort the meaning of law. When the meaning of law is distorted, the legitimacy of the court collapses.

The commercial nature of statutory courts becomes clear when you examine their outcomes. Many cases end with fines. These fines do not go to the injured party. They go to the institution. If no living soul has suffered loss, there is no natural reason for a payment. Yet statutory courts impose them as if they were a moral necessity. This reveals the true purpose of the process. A system that collects money through penalties is not a court of law. It is a revenue mechanism.

Revenue-based enforcement undermines trust. People feel the imbalance. They see that penalties are issued even when no one has been harmed. They see that courts prioritise codes over conscience. They see that institutions benefit financially from the process. This awareness causes people to question the fairness of the system. A court that causes its own loss of trust loses moral authority. When moral authority is lost, legitimacy follows.

Another sign of lost legitimacy is the behaviour of officials when jurisdiction is questioned. In a lawful court grounded in natural principles, every claim must be proven. Authority must be shown. Jurisdiction must be established. The court must demonstrate its standing before proceeding. Yet statutory courts avoid these questions. They respond with phrases that avoid the issue. They say things like, you are in the court, therefore the court has jurisdiction. They redirect attention. They issue warnings for asking simple questions. This behaviour exposes their dependence on assumption rather than truth.

A system that relies on assumption cannot claim legitimate authority. Assumption is not law. Assumption is not consent. Assumption is not justice. It is a tool used when a system cannot prove its claim. This is why statutory courts become uncomfortable when the living ask clear questions. They cannot show the lawful source of their authority, so they rely on intimidation. This intimidation appears in the form of raised voices, stern warnings, and threats of contempt. These responses have nothing to do with justice. They are attempts to preserve the illusion of power.

Fear is a tool used by systems that lack legitimacy. Fear keeps people compliant. Fear prevents questions. Fear turns living authority into submission. Yet fear only works when people believe the system holds power over them. When people recognise that authority begins with the living, fear dissolves. They see officials as men and women performing roles. They see courts as buildings with administrative staff. They see procedures as instructions written by institutions. They see the entire structure for what it is, not what it claims to be.

A statutory court uses the legal fiction to create a boundary between the institution and the living. The fiction absorbs the penalties. The fiction absorbs the accusations. The fiction is treated as if it were the responsible party. This separation is convenient for the system. It allows institutions to enforce commercial rules without confronting the natural rights of the living. Yet this separation becomes a weakness when the living refuse to identify as the fiction. When a man stands as himself, not as the entity on paper, the court struggles to continue. When a woman asserts her natural standing, the assumed jurisdiction starts to collapse.

The system attempts to conceal this by insisting that a name on a document represents the living. They say the two are the same. They say the fiction is the individual. They say the entity written in capital letters must answer. Yet these statements have no natural basis. A name is not a living soul. A name is not flesh and blood. A name is a symbol. It is used for convenience, not authority. When courts insist that the symbol overrides the living being, they abandon natural law entirely. A court that abandons natural law cannot claim legitimacy.

Another aspect of statutory courts that exposes their lost legitimacy is their selective application of law. They enforce certain rules with strict precision and ignore others completely. They act quickly when revenue is involved. They act slowly when institutions are challenged. They treat the living as accountable but shield corporations and government bodies from responsibility. This selective behaviour reveals a bias that undermines the idea of fairness. A court that enforces rules unequally cannot be legitimate.

True law applies equally to all living souls. It does not favour institutions. It does not protect officials. It does not give corporations special status. When a system treats institutions as superior to the people, it breaks the foundation of justice. It places power above truth. It places authority above honour. This inversion weakens the trust of the public. Trust is the lifeblood of lawful authority. When trust dies, the system loses its moral base.

Statutory courts also avoid addressing fraud when institutions commit it. They protect officials who act outside honour. They ignore misconduct. They dismiss challenges. They refuse to acknowledge harm caused by government departments. This behaviour reveals a system designed to maintain institutional power rather than protect the people. A court that protects wrongful acts committed by institutions while punishing ordinary citizens loses its credibility. It shows that the court is not independent. It is part of the same structure.

Another weakness appears in the way statutory courts rely on silence. Silence is taken as agreement. Failure to challenge assumptions is taken as consent. Yet true law requires explicit agreement, not presumed acceptance. The idea that silence equals consent benefits institutions, not the people. This approach turns courts into traps for the uninformed. A lawful system would never rely on silence. It would seek clear understanding. It would prioritise truth over procedure. It would value clarity over assumption.

A statutory court has also moved away from transparency. Much of the process happens behind closed doors. Decisions are made in chambers. Administrative staff handle vital documents. Judges consult private guidelines. These hidden processes remove the people from their rightful oversight role. In a community grounded in common law, justice is open. Everyone sees the process. Everyone hears the arguments. Everyone understands what is happening. Transparency builds legitimacy. Secrecy destroys it.

Statutory courts surround themselves with formality to create the appearance of legitimacy. Formality does not create authority. Authority comes from the living. When a court acts in ways that contradict natural principles, its formality becomes decoration rather than substance. A robe cannot create honour. A crest cannot establish truth. A procedure cannot produce justice. Only the living can do that.

As more people recognise the gap between statutory procedure and natural law, the authority of statutory courts continues to weaken. The system cannot regain legitimacy through force, intimidation, or symbolism. It can only regain legitimacy by returning to truth, aligning with natural principles, and recognising the authority of the people. Until that happens, statutory courts remain administrative venues pretending to be courts of law.

The people are remembering their role. They see the difference between genuine justice and administrative enforcement. They recognise that true courts do not serve institutions. They serve the living. They see that legitimacy comes from truth, not from titles. As this awareness grows, statutory courts continue to lose the authority they claim. Nothing can replace natural law. Nothing can override the living. Authority begins and ends with the people.

THE RISE OF THE STRAWMAN IN MODERN COURTS

The modern system speaks to a name, not a living soul. This is the core of the deception. Statutory courts, government departments, councils, and agencies operate as if the name written on their documents is the person. They do not recognise the living man. They do not acknowledge the living woman. They interact with a construct created on paper. This construct is the legal fiction. Many call it the strawman. It is the centrepiece of the system that has replaced natural law with commercial procedure.

The creation of the strawman is not explained openly. The system relies on silence and assumption. When a birth is registered, a record is created. That record is treated as the foundation of a legal identity. The name becomes an entry in a registry. Over time it becomes an entity used by the state to administer taxation, fines, licensing, and all forms of statutory control. The people assume this name and the living being are the same. They never question it, because the system trains them from childhood to accept this link as natural.

The link is not natural. It is administrative. It serves the system, not the living. The legal fiction allows institutions to deal with individuals as commercial entities. When a notice is issued, it is addressed to the fiction. When a demand is created, it is directed at the fiction. When a penalty is imposed, it is imposed on the fiction. Yet the system expects the living to act as surety. This is where the deception holds its power. The living take responsibility for the obligations of the fiction because they do not understand the separation.

In natural law, only the living can act. Only the living can speak. Only the living can enter agreements. A fiction cannot. It has no voice. It has no breath. It has no conscience. Yet statutory courts treat the fiction as if it were the responsible party. This shift allows the system to treat justice as a process of administration. The living are dragged into that process by their unchallenged acceptance of the fiction. Once they answer to the name on the document, the system assumes the contract is complete.

The court will never tell you this. It will never say its power depends on the fiction. It will never explain the difference between the living soul and the legal identity. It will never admit that its jurisdiction is commercial, not natural. Instead, it speaks in terms that obscure the truth. It says things like you must answer to the name. It says failure to respond is an offence. It says ignoring the notice creates consequences. These statements create the impression of authority, but the authority only exists if the living continues to act on behalf of the fiction.

This relationship between the fiction and the living did not appear overnight. It developed slowly as governments expanded their role. They created records for administrative control. They created identities for tracking, taxation, and regulation. Each generation accepted more paperwork. Each generation accepted more roles. The fiction grew stronger because the people believed the fiction represented them. Over time they forgot the difference between the living being and the entity on paper.

The growth of the strawman allowed institutions to move further away from natural justice. Courts could now address documents instead of people. They could process cases without needing an injured party. They could issue penalties where no harm existed. They could treat offences against regulations as if they were crimes. This structure made it possible to create entire industries around enforcement. Councils began issuing penalties for revenue. Agencies began imposing sanctions without injury. Police began enforcing codes rather than responding to harm. The legal fiction gave them the foundation to behave this way.

A living man cannot be compelled to follow a corporate procedure unless he consents. A legal fiction can. A living woman cannot be forced into a contract she did not agree to. A legal fiction can. This difference is the reason the system pushes the fiction at every opportunity. It gives institutions control. It gives courts the ability to operate commercially. It gives authorities a method to bypass natural law. This bypass is the core function of statutory courts.

The fiction allows the system to avoid honour. Honour belongs to the living. It cannot be applied to a construct. When a court deals with the fiction, it avoids facing the natural soul behind it. It avoids natural duty. It avoids the limitations that natural law places upon authority. A fiction cannot challenge jurisdiction. A fiction cannot demand proof. A fiction cannot assert natural standing. The system uses this to its advantage. It treats the fiction as if it were subordinate and expects the living to accept that subordination.

The separation becomes clear when a man refuses to act as the fiction. The court reacts with confusion. Officials become uneasy. The process slows down. They cannot proceed lawfully because their assumed jurisdiction collapses. They ask the man to confirm his name. They insist he must act for the fiction. They repeat the name on the document as if repetition creates authority. This behaviour reveals the weakness of the system. If their authority were natural, they would not need confirmation. They would not need assumption. They would not need consent.

The fiction also allows the system to maintain distance between officials and the people. When an institution issues a penalty, no living soul takes responsibility for the claim. The notice is produced by a system, not a person. The individual enforcing it hides behind policy. The official issuing it hides behind procedure. The court processing it hides behind rules. This distance protects institutions from accountability. It removes the requirement of honour. It creates a world where actions are taken without personal responsibility.

In natural law, responsibility is direct. If you cause harm, you answer for it as the living soul. You cannot hide behind a department. You cannot blame your role. You cannot pass responsibility to a system. You accept the consequences because honour demands it. A legal fiction cannot do this. It cannot feel responsibility. It cannot apologise. It cannot repair harm. Yet statutory courts treat the fiction as the party that must answer. This disconnect destroys the foundation of legitimate justice.

The rise of the strawman has allowed institutions to create a shadow world of obligations. These obligations do not exist in natural law. They exist only within the commercial system. Licensing fees. Regulatory fines. Penalty notices. Statutory charges. These demands are all directed at the fiction. They only bind the living when the living act on behalf of the fiction. The system does not need to prove harm because the fiction is treated as if it has obligations simply by existing.

Many people feel trapped by this structure. They sense that something is wrong. They do not understand why they are punished when no one has been injured. They do not understand why courts focus on paperwork rather than truth. They do not understand why officials can make claims without accountability. They do not realise that the foundation of the system is the fiction, not the living. Once this is understood, everything becomes clear.

The living still hold the highest authority. Natural law still stands above statute. The fiction only functions when the living forgets their standing. When a man remembers he is not the name on the document, the system loses power. When a woman speaks as herself rather than the fiction, institutions struggle to enforce claims. When a community recognises the difference between the living and the legal identity, the entire structure of statutory control weakens.

The rise of the strawman explains why statutory courts no longer resemble courts of law. They resemble administrative offices. They resemble commercial venues. They resolve paperwork, not disputes. They enforce compliance, not justice. They answer to institutions, not to the people. Once you understand the fiction, you understand why. A commercial system requires commercial entities. The strawman provides that entity.

The system depends on the strawman because it allows control without open conflict. If institutions attempted to place direct authority over the living, the people would reject it. A living soul does not submit easily to control. A living soul questions authority. A living soul demands truth. A living soul recognises injustice. The fiction does none of these things. It accepts every demand placed upon it because it has no consciousness. It cannot oppose. It cannot speak. It cannot refuse. This is why the system prefers the fiction. It gives institutions a path to act without facing the natural rights of the people.

The fiction also allows the system to expand its reach endlessly. There is no limit to the rules, codes, regulations, and procedures they can apply to a commercial entity. New obligations can be created at any time. New penalties can be introduced. New restrictions can be added. None of this requires harm, loss, or fraud. None of it requires natural justification. The fiction exists inside a commercial world where anything can be regulated. Institutions create more rules because each rule strengthens their control over the fiction. The living become caught in the net when they act as that fiction.

This commercial world has been built slowly. It did not replace natural law in a single moment. It grew layer by layer. First came the idea that the state needed records. Then came the idea that identities should be managed. After that came registration, licensing, certification, taxation, and the endless system of statutory obligations. Each new layer was accepted because people thought it was necessary. They did not see that these layers were being placed on the fiction, not the living. They accepted them because they believed the fiction and the living were the same.

The fiction made it possible for governments to treat people as assets. Assets can be monitored. Assets can be taxed. Assets can be controlled. A living soul cannot be treated in this way without consent. A fiction can. Over time institutions built an entire financial structure around the fiction. Documents represent value. Names carry debt. Records become proof of obligation. The living unknowingly stand behind these obligations as surety, because they do not realise the separation.

The system will never acknowledge this separation openly. If they did, their authority would collapse. The statutory court would lose its jurisdiction. Government departments would lose their enforcement power. Councils would lose their revenue streams. Agencies would lose their ability to control behaviour through regulation. Everything they do relies on the assumption that the fiction and the living are one and the same. Without that assumption, their structure cannot stand.

You can see the cracks in the system when people assert their natural standing. When someone refuses to act as the fiction, the system becomes unsettled. Officials repeat the name on the document as if repetition will force acceptance. They insist that the living must confirm they are the fiction. They claim the process cannot continue unless the person answers to the name. These behaviours show that their authority is not grounded in law, but in the assumption that the person will act as the fiction.

A court grounded in natural law would never need such tactics. It would address the living directly. It would recognise the individual as the source of authority. It would require evidence of harm or loss. It would honour the principles of truth and fairness. It would never rely on confusion to establish jurisdiction. The statutory court relies on confusion because it cannot prove jurisdiction through natural principles. It must use assumption. It must use silence. It must use psychological pressure.

The rise of the strawman explains why statutory courts use language that feels unnatural. They speak in terms designed for commercial procedure. They use titles such as defendant, claimant, applicant, and respondent. These words describe roles within the fiction, not the living. When the living accepts these titles, they step into the commercial process. This shift transforms the interaction into a contractual arrangement. The living becomes a participant in a system that does not serve natural justice.

The fiction also allows institutions to issue commands without accountability. A notice addressed to the fiction requires no living person to stand behind the claim. The institution sends the notice. The court enforces it. The police act upon it. No living soul accepts responsibility for its creation. This lack of responsibility breaks the chain of honour that natural law requires. If a man accuses another of wrongdoing, he must face the accused. He must provide evidence. He must accept the consequences if his claim is false. The fiction removes these duties. It removes honour from the process entirely.

Honour cannot be removed without consequence. When a system operates without honour, it loses its legitimacy. When officials hide behind roles, they lose their accountability. When courts hide behind procedure, they lose their moral authority. When institutions hide behind the fiction, they lose their connection to the people. A system that loses honour cannot survive unless it replaces honour with force, fear, and manipulation. That is the direction statutory courts have taken.

The fiction also allows the system to create fear through penalties. Penalties appear threatening only when the living believes the fiction must comply. When a man stands in natural law, the penalty loses power. It is directed at a commercial entity. The living is not bound by it unless he consents. The system knows this. That is why it pressures people to respond. If the fiction is ignored and the living refuses to engage, the system struggles to enforce its claims. Its only remaining tool is intimidation.

Intimidation appears in many forms. Threats of additional charges. Warnings of enforcement action. Letters claiming serious consequences. The system sends these documents to frighten the living into acting as the fiction. If the living steps into the role, the contract becomes active. If the living refuses, the system cannot proceed lawfully. This truth is hidden behind layers of official language, yet it remains the foundation of the system.

Understanding the fiction brings clarity to every part of statutory enforcement. When you see a notice addressed to the fiction, you understand it is not directed at the living. When you see a demand for payment based on a regulation, you understand it applies to the commercial entity, not natural law. When you see a court summons, you recognise it as an invitation to enter a commercial process. These interpretations restore power to the living. They remove fear. They reveal the system for what it is.

The fiction also explains why statutory courts do not require an injured party. They can proceed without harm because they are not dealing with the living. They are dealing with a commercial entity. Commercial entities do not require harm or loss to be liable. They only require a breach of terms. Statutory codes function as commercial terms. If the fiction breaches a code, the system creates a penalty. The living becomes responsible for the penalty only when they accept the role of surety.

This shift to commercial procedure explains why statutory courts do not resemble community courts. A community court operates through honour. It involves the people directly. It requires accountability from all sides. It respects natural rights. A statutory court does none of these things. It processes paperwork. It enforces codes. It protects institutions. It ignores natural principles. It exists to manage the fiction, not to serve the living.

When you understand the rise of the strawman, the behaviour of statutory courts becomes predictable. They are not acting unlawfully according to their own structure. They are acting commercially. They are managing contracts. They are processing obligations. They are enforcing terms. Their system makes sense only when viewed from the perspective of the fiction. It makes no sense from the perspective of natural law, which is why so many people feel trapped, confused, and mistreated.

The path back to natural authority begins with recognising the separation. The living must understand they are not the fiction. They must understand they are not the name. They must understand they do not automatically consent to commercial procedures. Once this understanding returns, the people can stand on natural law again. They can speak as themselves. They can refuse roles that do not apply to them. They can demand honour from institutions. They can hold officials accountable. They can rebuild courts grounded in truth.

The fiction has no power over the living unless the living gives it life. This is the heart of the matter. The system controls through illusion. Once the illusion is seen for what it is, the people reclaim their authority. They stand as sovereign souls. They step away from commercial jurisdiction. They form courts that reflect natural principles. They choose sheriffs who uphold honour. They create structures that serve the living, not the fiction.

WHAT A COMMON LAW COURT IS

A common law court is the natural expression of authority held by the people. It is not created by statute. It is not granted permission by any government. It does not operate under corporate rules. It exists because the living hold the power to resolve disputes, protect peace, and uphold honour. This power is older than any institution. It comes from nature. It comes from truth. It comes from the simple fact that law begins with life, not with government.

The common law court is not a building. It is not an organisation. It is not an agency. It is a gathering of living men and women standing together to resolve matters according to natural principles. Its legitimacy does not come from documents or offices. Its legitimacy comes from the people who form it. When a community gathers in honour, the court is formed. When the community listens, the court is active. When the community reaches a decision grounded in truth, the court speaks with lawful authority.

This authority belongs to the people because the people are the source of law. No institution can create higher authority than that. Governments can only create statutes. Councils can only create regulations. Agencies can only create policies. None of these have natural force. None of them outrank the living. None of them override the principles of harm, loss, and fraud. A statute can instruct the fiction, but it cannot command the living without consent. A common law court operates beyond the limits of statute because it does not require consent. It already stands on natural truth.

A common law court focuses on the only three principles that matter in genuine law. Harm. Loss. Fraud. If a case does not involve one of these, it does not belong in the court. There is no role for policy breaches. There is no room for administrative offences. There is no place for corporate demands. A man who has harmed another must repair the harm. A woman who has caused loss must restore what was taken. A person who has deceived another must face the consequences. These are the only true violations. Anything outside these principles is instruction, not law.

This clarity is what separates a common law court from a statutory court. A statutory court begins with paperwork. It examines documents before it examines truth. It operates on procedure before it considers fairness. It follows rules before it acknowledges reason. A common law court begins with the people. It hears their words. It listens to the injured. It questions with honesty. It weighs facts rather than forms. It prioritises truth above every other factor.

The structure of a common law court is simple and direct. The people gather. They choose a foreman from among themselves. The foreman guides the process. The parties speak. Witnesses speak. The community listens. There is no hierarchy. There is no judge removed from the people. There is no elevated bench. The people are equal because authority is shared. This equality removes intimidation. It removes manipulation. It removes the sense that one person controls the process.

In a common law court, the living can speak freely. They are not bound by the roles imposed by statutory courts. They do not become defendants or claimants. They remain themselves. They speak as the living soul. They speak in honour. Their standing is clear. This clarity removes the confusion that statutory courts rely upon. A statutory court uses titles to draw the living into commercial roles. A common law court rejects these roles entirely. It deals with the living, not the fiction.

Evidence in a common law court is based on truth, not compliance. The people accept testimony that is given in honour. They consider facts presented without deception. They recognise the weight of an oath spoken by a living soul. They do not rely on documents unless the documents support truth. Written statements are not superior to spoken truth. Official records are not superior to direct testimony. The people consider everything carefully and decide based on fairness.

This approach reflects natural justice. Natural justice does not require elaborate rules. It requires sincerity. It requires openness. It requires accountability. When the people hear the truth, they recognise it. When they hear deception, they recognise that too. Natural justice works because it relies on conscience, not technicality. A statutory court hides behind technicalities because it cannot rely on conscience. It processes cases mechanically. It follows rules that often contradict truth. It prioritises procedure rather than fairness. This is why statutory courts feel unnatural. They have replaced truth with process.

A common law court restores the proper order. It gives the people back their rightful place as arbiters of justice. It gives communities the ability to repair harm directly. It removes the needless involvement of institutions that do not serve the living. It places responsibility where it belongs. The living hold authority. The living uphold honour. The living reach decisions. The living enforce outcomes. This is the natural flow of justice.

The role of the jury is central in a common law court. The jury is not a tool of the state. It is the voice of the community. It does not follow instructions from institutions. It follows the principles of truth, fairness, and natural law. The jury listens. It weighs evidence. It decides as a collective body. Its decision is grounded in shared understanding, not in statutory guidelines. A common law jury does not need legal training. It only needs conscience and clarity.

The common law court recognises that justice belongs to everyone. It does not place power in the hands of experts. It does not depend on the approval of government. It does not require people to surrender their rights. Instead, it invites the people to take responsibility. It invites them to become active participants in their own protection. This participation strengthens communities. It builds trust. It creates peace. A community that holds its own court becomes resilient. It becomes confident. It becomes independent from systems that no longer act with honour.

Another defining feature of a common law court is transparency. Everything occurs in the open. There is no hidden process. There are no private hearings. There are no secret decisions. Justice must be visible to be legitimate. When people witness the process, they trust it. When they trust it, they support it. When they support it, the court gains strength. Transparency removes corruption. It removes manipulation. It removes the ability for individuals to misuse authority. A common law court thrives on openness because truth thrives in the open.

A common law court also respects the concept of notice. Notice is fundamental in natural law. People cannot be held accountable for anything they were not aware of. A statute assumes notice simply because it is written. A common law court rejects this assumption. It understands that lawful notice must be clear, personal, and acknowledged. Notice must be given by the living and received by the living. Without notice, there is no agreement. Without agreement, there is no obligation.

This approach reinforces consent. Consent is the cornerstone of natural authority. A man cannot be bound without his consent. A woman cannot be obligated without agreement. A community cannot be controlled without acceptance. A common law court respects this truth. It does not impose authority. It recognises authority. It honours the natural right of individuals to withhold consent when something is unjust.

Natural justice requires balance. A common law court seeks balance, not punishment. Punishment serves institutions, not communities. Balance restores peace. If harm occurs, the court resolves it. If loss occurs, the court repairs it. If fraud occurs, the court exposes it. The goal is restoration, not domination. This is why common law courts focus on remedy rather than penalty. They understand that justice is the restoration of order, not the imposition of power.

A common law court is an expression of collective honour. Honour binds the process together. Without honour, natural law cannot function. Honour ensures that those involved speak truthfully. Honour ensures that decisions are fair. Honour ensures that outcomes reflect justice. Honour ensures that authority is exercised responsibly. In a statutory court, honour is replaced with compliance. Compliance does not require truth. Compliance requires submission. This is the difference between a lawful court and a corporate court.

A common law court reminds the people that law is theirs. It does not belong to institutions. It does not belong to governments. It does not belong to corporations. It belongs to the living. The living create law by living it. They enforce it by standing in honour. They protect it by supporting each other. A statutory court depends on obedience. A common law court depends on truth. One belongs to institutions. The other belongs to the people.

A common law court exists wherever the people gather in honour to resolve a matter. It is not tied to a building because buildings do not create authority. It is not tied to uniforms because uniforms do not create truth. It is not tied to paperwork because paperwork does not create justice. Authority flows from the living. When the living assemble and agree to hear a dispute, the court is formed. This approach makes common law courts powerful, because their power does not depend on anything external. It rises from within the people themselves.

The purpose of a common law court is to restore peace. Peace is the natural state of a community living in truth. Peace is not the absence of conflict. It is the presence of honour. Honour creates stability. Honour prevents harm. Honour resolves disputes quickly and fairly. A court that respects honour does not seek victory for one side. It seeks balance. Balance heals the community. Balance strengthens relationships. Balance prevents further harm. This is why common law courts are centred on remedy, not punishment.

Punishment is an invention of statutory systems. It benefits institutions, not communities. Punishment generates revenue. Punishment reinforces control. Punishment deepens fear. Communities that rely on punishment lose their unity. They become dependent on external authority to enforce order. In such communities, people no longer resolve disputes themselves. They hand those disputes to institutions. This transfer weakens natural authority and gives institutions power they were never meant to hold.

A common law court returns responsibility to the people. When responsibility returns, authority returns. When authority returns, accountability returns. These three elements form the core of natural justice. A man who stands before a common law court does not face domination. He faces truth. He faces his community. He faces his own actions. This creates genuine accountability, something statutory systems avoid. Statutory systems treat people as case numbers. A common law court treats them as living souls.

The openness of a common law court exposes falsehood quickly. Deception cannot survive in a space where the people speak directly and without fear. A statutory court hides behind procedure, allowing false claims to pass if the paperwork is correct. A common law court requires truth, not form. It requires sincerity, not legal tricks. It requires clarity, not confusion. In this environment honesty becomes the strongest form of defence, and dishonesty becomes the quickest path to exposure.

Another defining feature of the common law court is its flexibility. Because it is grounded in natural law, not statute, it can adapt to any situation without losing legitimacy. Natural law is constant, but its application can vary depending on the context. The people understand this because they live within the situation. They can weigh the facts. They can consider intent. They can examine circumstances. This flexible approach leads to fair outcomes that reflect the needs of the community rather than the demands of institutions.

Statutory courts cannot adapt. They follow strict rules that often produce unfair results. They punish without considering intent. They ignore context. They enforce penalties even when there is no harm. Their rigid structure may look orderly, but it produces injustice because it ignores the human element. A common law court remains lawful because it remains human. It has not surrendered its soul to bureaucracy.

A common law court does not rely on representation. The living speak for themselves. They do not need experts to interpret their words. They do not need legal professionals to speak on their behalf. They do not need intermediaries to convert their truth into technical language. Representation weakens the individual because it implies they cannot speak for themselves. It creates distance between the living soul and the court. It turns justice into a performance rather than a genuine inquiry.

In a common law court, the voice of the individual is respected. A man speaks his truth. A woman stands in honour. The community listens. This direct interaction strengthens the integrity of the process. It reminds the people that justice is not a service provided by institutions. It is a responsibility carried by the living. When people speak for themselves, the process stays grounded in authenticity. When they hand their voice to others, the process becomes artificial.

The simplicity of the common law court is one of its greatest strengths. Statutory systems use complexity as a shield. They hide behind long documents, numerous rules, and technical terms. This complexity discourages participation. It creates dependence. It isolates the people. A common law court removes these barriers. The rules are understood by all because they are based on conscience. The process is accessible to all because it is based on truth. The outcomes are accepted by all because they are based on fairness.

Because common law courts rely on the people, they empower the people. A community that resolves its own disputes becomes strong. It becomes self-reliant. It becomes independent from systems that do not serve its interests. This independence is not rebellion. It is the natural state of a free people. When communities become independent, statutory systems lose influence. They cannot control people who recognise their natural authority.

The strength of a common law court also comes from its oath. Oaths are not mere words. They are binding commitments made by living souls. When a foreman takes an oath to act in honour, he binds himself to truth. When a juror takes an oath to decide fairly, he binds himself to justice. These oaths create a moral foundation that cannot be replaced by paperwork. A statutory judge may follow rules, but rules do not create honour. Only conscience does. The oath in a common law court is a recognition of the responsibility carried by each participant.

Witnesses also take oaths. Their oath is a commitment to speak truthfully. This commitment carries weight because it is made before the community. In statutory courts, oaths have lost meaning. They are recited as routine. They are overshadowed by legal procedure. In a common law court, an oath remains powerful because it is grounded in natural law. A false oath is an act of dishonour. Dishonour has consequences. Not institutional penalties, but community accountability. This accountability reinforces trust in the process.

A common law court values restoration above everything else. When harm occurs, the focus is on repairing it, not punishing it. When loss occurs, the focus is on restoring what was taken. When fraud occurs, the focus is on correcting the deception and protecting the community. The goal is not to overpower the offender. The goal is to return balance. Balance repairs relationships. Balance prevents further disputes. Balance strengthens the community.

Statutory courts frame justice as a battle. One side wins. One side loses. Victory is often achieved through technical advantage rather than truth. This adversarial structure encourages manipulation. It encourages exploitation. It encourages dishonour. A common law court does not support these behaviours. It seeks cooperation, not conflict. It seeks truth, not victory. It seeks resolution, not dominance.

Another essential feature of a common law court is that it exists free from institutional influence. No government can interfere. No corporate body can direct its decisions. No official can control its process. A common law court belongs to the people. It is shaped by them, guided by them, and upheld by them. This independence ensures that justice is not corrupted by outside interests. It ensures that the process remains clean, fair, and grounded in truth.

Institutions fear this independence because they cannot manipulate a court that answers only to natural law. They cannot use common law courts to enforce revenue policies. They cannot use them to impose regulations. They cannot use them to control the population. A common law court stands outside institutional structures. It does not recognise authority that contradicts natural law. This is why institutions resist the return of common law. They know it exposes their limits.

Despite this resistance, common law courts continue to grow because the people recognise their value. People are tired of systems that punish without fairness. They are tired of courts that ignore harm. They are tired of institutions that claim authority without accountability. They are tired of being treated as fictions rather than living souls. A common law court gives them a place to be heard. It gives them a place to stand. It gives them a place where honour is recognised.

A common law court is more than a method of resolving disputes. It is a declaration of sovereignty. It is a reminder that the people hold the highest authority. It is an expression of natural law in action. It is a space where truth governs, not statute. It is a place where the living speak, not the fiction. It is a structure built on conscience, honour, and justice.

HOW A COMMON LAW COURT IS FORMED

A common law court begins with the people. It does not begin with government recognition. It does not begin with written authority from an institution. It does not begin with permission. Permission is a concept used by statutory systems to control. In natural law, the living do not ask for permission to uphold truth. A community forms a common law court the moment its members gather in honour to resolve a matter. That gathering, that agreement, that commitment to truth, creates the foundation of lawful authority.

The process starts with one question. Who is willing to stand in honour? A common law court cannot function without honour. Honour ensures that every participant acts truthfully and openly. Honour ensures that the outcome reflects justice rather than personal interest. Honour ensures that the people recognise their own authority and exercise it responsibly. When the people stand in honour, the court naturally forms around them.

Every common law court begins with an assembly. An assembly is a gathering of living men and women who agree to resolve a matter peacefully and fairly. The assembly does not need to be large. It can be a handful of people or an entire community. What matters is consent. Each person present consents to take part. Each person consents to hear the matter. Each person consents to uphold natural law. Consent is the bedrock of the court. Without consent, the gathering is not lawful. With consent, the gathering becomes a court.

Once the assembly forms, the next step is choosing a foreman. The foreman is not a judge. He does not sit above the people. He does not have special powers. He is a facilitator. His role is to guide the process, keep discussion orderly, and ensure that everyone has the opportunity to speak. The foreman is chosen by the people because he is trusted. Trust is essential. A foreman must be a man of honour, a person who values truth, fairness, and clarity. The people must willingly recognise him. A foreman who imposes himself holds no authority. A foreman accepted by the people holds lawful authority because they entrusted him with their consent.

The assembly also chooses a scribe or recorder. This individual documents the process. The record does not need to follow statutory formats. It needs only to reflect the truth. It must show who was present, what was discussed, what evidence was presented, and what decision was reached. This record becomes the written expression of the court. It is a statement of fact. It is not a corporate document. It is a truthful account created by the people. This account can be used later to show what occurred and to confirm the legitimacy of the court.

The parties involved in the dispute stand before the assembly. They do not become defendants or claimants. These are statutory labels used to draw the living into roles created for the fiction. In a common law court, the parties remain living men and women. They speak truthfully, not through legal representatives. They explain what happened in plain language. They are heard by their community, not by officials working for institutions. The removal of titles creates clarity. It removes the artificial hierarchy found in statutory courts. It reminds everyone that the process belongs to the people, not to a system.

Evidence is presented openly. There are no secret documents. No concealed files. No undisclosed witnesses. The people must see everything. Transparency is essential. It prevents corruption. It prevents manipulation. It prevents misunderstanding. Evidence can be spoken, written, or demonstrated. What matters is not the format but the truth. Evidence that is honest will be recognised by the assembly. Evidence that is deceptive will also be recognised. The people's collective experience allows them to distinguish between sincerity and falsehood in a way that statutory courts cannot.

Witnesses also speak in the presence of the assembly. They do not swear oaths to the state. They swear oaths to truth. An oath in a common law court is sacred because it binds the individual to honour. A man who lies under oath violates honour. A woman who lies under oath breaks trust. The consequences are not statutory penalties. The consequences are community accountability. Dishonour carries weight in a community that values truth. This accountability strengthens the process because people understand the importance of honesty.

The assembly then forms a jury. The jury can be selected from the members of the assembly or chosen beforehand. The key requirement is impartiality. A juror must be someone who can listen without bias. They must be someone who values fairness above personal preference. They must be someone who places truth above all else. A juror does not follow instructions from a judge. They follow conscience. Conscience guides their judgment. Conscience ensures that the decision reflects natural law rather than statutory rules.

The jury listens carefully to the evidence presented. They ask questions where needed. They discuss the matter openly with the assembly. Their goal is not to punish. Their goal is to determine truth. Truth is the foundation of their decision. When they reach a conclusion, it is based on whether harm, loss, or fraud occurred. If none of these exist, there is no case. If one or more of these exist, the jury decides what remedy is required. Remedy, not punishment, is the focus.

A common law court resolves disputes by restoring balance. If harm occurred, the person responsible must repair it. If loss occurred, the person responsible must make restitution. If fraud occurred, the deception must be corrected and the injured party protected. These remedies serve the community. They bring peace. They ensure that relationships can heal. They remind everyone that justice is not about domination. It is about restoration.

Once a decision is reached, the foreman speaks on behalf of the jury. He announces the decision clearly and openly. He explains the reasoning behind it. He confirms the remedy. This announcement carries lawful authority because it is grounded in natural law and supported by the people. A statutory court claims legitimacy through its structure. A common law court holds legitimacy through truth and consent.

The record of the court is then finalised by the scribe. The record reflects the process honestly. It includes the decision and the remedy required. This document becomes the written expression of the people's authority. It shows that the common law court acted in honour, heard the matter fairly, and resolved it according to natural principles. This record may be used if institutions attempt to interfere or challenge the legitimacy of the court. The record stands as evidence of lawful process.

The enforcement of a common law court decision is not domination. It is cooperation. The people support the remedy because they trust the process. They recognise the fairness of the decision. They uphold it because they value the principles that guide the court. In this context a common law sheriff may become involved, but his role is not force. His role is protection. He protects the peace. He ensures that the decision is respected. He represents the authority of the people.

A common law court is formed through consent, honour, truth, and community. These elements create stability. They create legitimacy. They create a lawful environment where disputes are resolved fairly. When the people form a court in this way, they exercise the authority they were born with. They reclaim their natural role as guardians of justice. They demonstrate that law belongs to them.

A common law court gains strength from the simplicity of its formation. It does not ask for external approval. It does not wait for recognition from the state. It does not rely on registration, licensing, or certification. These concepts belong to statutory systems. A lawful court under natural principles needs none of them. Its authority comes from the people who form it, and that authority is complete because natural law is complete. Every step in the formation of a common law court reflects this truth. The living create it. The living guide it. The living enforce it. No institution stands above the people.

A critical part of forming a common law court is understanding jurisdiction. Jurisdiction does not come from buildings, robes, or government declarations. Jurisdiction comes from consent. Consent is the foundation of authority. A man does not fall under the authority of a court unless he consents. A woman does not accept obligations unless she agrees to them. A community does not fall under external control unless it allows it. When the people form a common law court, they create a jurisdiction based on their consent. That consent is lawful because it is given by the living.

Consent in a common law court is not assumed. It is expressed. Those who take part agree openly. They stand in honour. They recognise the authority of natural law. They accept the responsibility that comes with participating in justice. This open expression of consent creates a lawful space where disputes can be resolved. In contrast, statutory courts rely on assumed consent. They take silence as agreement. They take appearance as acceptance. They take participation as submission. This difference shows why common law courts are lawful while statutory courts are administrative.

Once a common law court is formed through assembly and consent, notice becomes essential. Notice ensures fairness. Notice ensures transparency. Notice prevents surprise. Notice prevents deception. A man who is called to stand before the court must receive clear communication of the claim against him. That notice must come from a living soul. It must be delivered openly. It must be understood. It must give the individual time to prepare. Natural law does not allow hidden claims or secret allegations. Notice ensures that the process remains honourable.

After notice is served, the individual who is called before the court must be given the opportunity to respond. This opportunity is not a formality. It is a right. Natural justice requires that every soul be heard. Hearing both sides is essential to honour. A common law court cannot reach a decision without listening. Listening is the heart of justice. It brings clarity. It uncovers truth. It exposes falsehood. A community that listens acts lawfully because it respects the dignity of each individual.

When the assembly gathers to hear the response, the individual speaks in his own voice. She speaks in her own words. There is no need for representation. There is no need for technical language. There is no need for constructed arguments. The living speak plainly. This plainness removes confusion. It removes manipulation. It removes the layers of complexity that statutory courts rely on. When people speak directly, truth becomes easier to recognise.

A crucial aspect of forming a common law court is the absence of hierarchy. Hierarchy creates imbalance. It creates opportunities for domination. It creates a sense of superiority in those who claim positions of authority. A common law court has no such structure. The foreman guides the process, but he does not rule it. The jury makes the decision, but they do not act above the people. The assembly provides oversight, but it does not impose personal beliefs. Everyone participates as equals. Equality creates legitimacy. Equality keeps the process grounded in natural principles.

This equality also extends to the handling of evidence. Evidence is not filtered through procedural rules. It is not accepted or rejected based on technical requirements. It is examined on its merits. The people decide whether evidence is truthful. They decide whether it is relevant. They decide whether it supports the claim. This approach creates fairness because the goal is understanding, not conformity to technical procedure. Statutory courts reject evidence based on rules crafted to protect institutions. Common law courts accept evidence that reflects reality.

The decision-making process in a common law court takes place through open discussion. The jury does not withdraw into a closed room. They do not deliberate in secret. They do not hide their reasoning. The people are present. They see the process. They understand the steps. This openness prevents corruption. It prevents manipulation. It prevents coercion. When decisions are made openly, the community can trust the result. This transparency is what gives a common law court its legitimacy.

Once the jury reaches a conclusion, it is expressed through remedy. Remedy reflects natural law. It restores balance. It repairs harm. It corrects loss. It exposes deception. Remedy is not punishment. Punishment belongs to systems that seek control rather than justice. Punishment creates fear. Punishment damages communities. Punishment serves institutions. Remedy heals. Remedy strengthens. Remedy reflects honour. A community that focuses on remedy becomes strong.

The enforcement of remedy in a common law court is carried out with the same commitment to honour that guides the rest of the process. Enforcement is not coercion. Enforcement is cooperation. When the people agree on a remedy, they support it because they recognise it as just. They encourage the individual responsible to honour his duty. If that individual refuses, the community has the authority to insist. This insistence is not force. It is the collective voice of the people. The common law sheriff, if appointed, ensures that this process remains peaceful and lawful.

The role of the common law sheriff becomes relevant at this stage. The sheriff is the peace officer of the people. He is not an enforcer of penalties. He is not an arm of the state. He is not a policy officer. His primary duty is to protect the peace. He ensures that the remedy is carried out in a fair and honourable way. He prevents escalation. He prevents intimidation. He prevents actions that could harm the community. His authority comes from the people, not from institutions.

The presence of a sheriff reflects the natural structure of a lawful community. Communities have always needed individuals who act as guardians of peace. These individuals were chosen because they were known for their integrity. They were not granted authority from above. They were recognised from within. The modern common law sheriff follows the same tradition. His authority flows directly from the people he serves. This authority is lawful because it is rooted in consent and honour.

A common law court continues to exist for as long as the assembly recognises it. Its authority is ongoing. Its decisions remain valid. Its record stands as evidence of lawful judgment. The court dissolves naturally once the matter is resolved, but the authority of the people remains. A common law court can be formed again whenever needed. There is no restriction on when or where it may arise. Every community holds this power.

The strength of a common law court comes from its purity. It is not corrupted by politics. It is not influenced by money. It is not shaped by institutions. It is shaped by truth, honour, conscience, and fairness. These elements make it lawful. These elements make it legitimate. These elements make it unshakeable even when institutions attempt to challenge it. A statutory court may ignore natural law, but natural law does not depend on recognition. It stands with or without the system.

A community that knows how to form a common law court becomes independent. It gains the ability to protect itself. It gains the ability to resolve disputes without surrendering authority to institutions. It gains the ability to stand in honour. Once a community experiences this, it does not return to statutory dependence. The people feel the difference. They feel the clarity. They feel the fairness. They feel the strength that comes from acting in truth.

A common law court is not a novelty or an imitation. It is the original court of the people. It is the natural expression of living authority. It is the true foundation of justice. Every community has the right to form one. Every living soul has the right to stand before one. Every dispute involving harm, loss, or fraud can be resolved through one. This is natural law in action.

THE ROLE OF A COMMON LAW SHERIFF

A common law sheriff is the guardian of the people's peace. He is not an officer of the state. He is not controlled by statutory codes. He does not enforce corporate policy. His authority comes from the living, and because it comes from the living, it sits above any authority claimed by institutions. A sheriff chosen by the people carries a duty that begins with honour, not power. He stands between the community and any force that attempts to interfere unlawfully with their rights.

In natural law a sheriff exists because communities need peace, not control. Peace is created when people live in truth. Control is created when institutions impose their will. The common law sheriff serves peace, not control. His duty is to protect the natural rights of every man and woman in the community. He lives among them. He knows them. They trust him because his authority comes from their consent, not from a document issued by a government department.

A sheriff under common law represents the living. A statutory officer represents the state. This difference shapes everything he does. A statutory officer enforces rules created by institutions. These rules may or may not reflect natural law. They may serve revenue. They may serve political agendas. They may serve corporate interests. A common law sheriff enforces only one set of principles. Do no harm. Cause no loss. Commit no fraud. These principles define natural law. They define honour. They define justice.

This alignment with natural law makes the authority of a common law sheriff more legitimate than any authority claimed by statutory officers. A statutory officer may hold a badge, but a badge does not create honour. A sheriff holds the trust of the people, and trust is more powerful than symbols. A statutory officer may carry documents issued by councils or government agencies, but documents do not create natural authority. A sheriff carries the consent of the community, and consent is the foundation of all lawful authority.

The people choose the sheriff. They choose him because he is known for integrity. They choose him because he speaks truthfully. They choose him because he acts fairly. They choose him because he places honour above personal interest. A sheriff who loses honour loses authority. The people can withdraw their consent at any time. This accountability ensures that the sheriff remains a protector, not a ruler. His power is limited by natural law and guided by conscience.

A sheriff's oath is central to his role. His oath is not sworn to a monarch. It is not sworn to a government. It is not sworn to a department. It is sworn to truth, natural law, and the people he serves. This oath binds him to act with integrity. It binds him to protect life, property, and peace. It binds him to stand firm against unlawful interference. It binds him to defend the rights of the living. It binds him to uphold the decisions of the common law court. His oath carries weight because it is spoken as a living man, not as a representative of a corporation.

Because the sheriff stands on natural law, he does not operate as an enforcer. He operates as a protector. Enforcement belongs to statutory systems that rely on fear and punishment. Protection belongs to natural law. When harm occurs, the sheriff helps ensure that remedy is carried out. When disputes escalate, he intervenes to restore calm. When institutions attempt to trespass against the people, he stands between them and the community. This protective role is lawful because the people entrusted him with that duty.

A sheriff must be able to recognise the difference between lawful authority and unlawful interference. Lawful authority is grounded in natural law. It protects life. It respects property. It requires consent. It acts only where harm, loss, or fraud exist. Unlawful interference hides behind procedure. It relies on intimidation. It ignores natural rights. It operates without consent. A sheriff who understands this distinction becomes the shield of the community. He prevents institutions from overstepping their rightful limits.

When government officials, council officers, or enforcement agents attempt to impose claims without natural justification, the sheriff intervenes. He asks for proof of authority. He asks for evidence of harm. He asks for lawful justification. He does not accept threats. He does not accept assumptions. He does not accept titles as authority. He evaluates the situation through natural law. If no harm, loss, or fraud exists, the interference is unlawful. The sheriff then protects the individual targeted by the institution.

A sheriff must also understand consent. Consent is the cornerstone of lawful interaction. No individual can be bound without consent. No contract can exist without agreement. No jurisdiction can apply without acceptance. When institutions claim authority, the sheriff examines whether consent exists. If consent is absent, their authority collapses. If consent is withdrawn, their jurisdiction ends. This is why the sheriff stands as the guardian of consent. He ensures that no one is forced into obligations they did not choose.

A common law sheriff does not rely on force. Force is the tool of statutory systems. Natural law does not require force. It requires clarity. It requires truth. It requires honour. A sheriff who stands calmly and confidently in honour carries more authority than any statutory officer who carries force. A statutory officer may attempt to intimidate. He may use threats or coercion. But threats collapse when the living stand firmly on natural law. The sheriff embodies this firmness. His calm presence reminds institutions that they cannot overpower truth.

The sheriff also serves as the protector of the common law court. A court formed by the people stands outside the control of the state. This independence threatens institutions that rely on statutory authority. When institutions attempt to challenge the court, the sheriff stands between them and the assembly. He does not allow unlawful interference. He ensures the people can gather freely. He ensures that cases can be heard without disruption. He ensures that the authority of natural law is respected.

A statutory officer may claim he has the right to intervene, yet those claims depend on statutes, not natural law. Statutes do not outrank the people. Statutes do not override consent. Statutes do not grant authority over the living. A sheriff who knows this cannot be swayed by statutory claims. He understands that natural law is higher. He understands that only harm, loss, and fraud create lawful authority. He understands that institutions must prove jurisdiction, not assume it. This understanding protects the court from unlawful intrusion.

A common law sheriff must be steady. He must remain calm when confronted by aggression. He must remain firm when faced with intimidation. He must remain honourable even when others act without honour. His strength does not come from physical power. It comes from the community that stands behind him. It comes from natural law. It comes from truth. Institutions fear this strength because they cannot control it.

The sheriff also acts as a witness. Because he is trusted by the people, his presence carries weight. When he observes a dispute, he records facts. When he sees harm, he reports truthfully. When he sees deception, he exposes it. His word is respected because it is grounded in honour. This makes him an essential part of maintaining peace in the community. People know that he will act fairly. They know he will not take sides without cause. They know he will not allow falsehood to take root.

The sheriff may also be called upon to deliver notices on behalf of the common law court. Notice is a vital part of natural justice. A sheriff delivers notice because notice must come from the living. A letter sent by an institution does not carry the same weight. A notice delivered by a sheriff carries honour because it is delivered openly, clearly, and personally. The sheriff ensures that the individual receiving the notice understands its contents. He ensures that the process remains lawful.

The authority of the sheriff grows with the strength of the community. When the people stand together, the sheriff's position becomes unshakeable. When the people forget their natural authority, the sheriff weakens. This balance reveals the truth. The sheriff does not rule the people. The people empower the sheriff. His position only exists because the people choose it. His authority only stands because the people recognise it. His power only holds because the people uphold natural law.

A common law sheriff represents the highest peace authority within a community because he stands on natural law, not statutory power. His authority cannot be bought. It cannot be issued. It cannot be granted by institutions. It must come from the people. When the people recognise a man as their sheriff, they are expressing trust in him as the guardian of their rights. This trust is not symbolic. It is lawful. It is the foundation that strengthens his role and gives him the ability to act when peace is threatened.

A sheriff must understand that his role is rooted in accountability. Accountability ensures that he always acts within honour. If he behaves without honour, the community can remove him. This removal is lawful because his authority came from the people in the first place. A man who misuses the position loses the trust that gave him authority. This safeguard protects the community. It prevents corruption. It ensures that the sheriff remains a protector rather than an enforcer.

Because the sheriff operates on natural law, his authority extends to any situation where harm, loss, or fraud is present. He does not need written permission to intervene. He does not wait for orders. He does not follow commands from institutions. He responds when peace is threatened. This responsiveness makes his authority practical. If a dispute becomes dangerous, he steps in. If a man's property is threatened, he protects it. If a woman is treated without honour, he upholds her rights. His presence stabilises situations because people recognise that he acts for the community rather than an external system.

One of the most important duties of a common law sheriff is to protect individuals from unlawful interference by institutions. Institutions often act under the assumption that their policies outrank natural law. Councils issue demands. Enforcement officers attempt to seize property. Government agents issue notices based on regulations rather than harm. These actions rely on fear and confusion. They rely on the belief that the institution holds authority over the living. A sheriff who stands in natural law challenges this belief directly.

When an official attempts to act without natural justification, the sheriff intervenes. He asks a simple question. Where is the authority? If the official cannot show evidence of harm, loss, or fraud, the interference is unlawful. The sheriff can prevent it. He can instruct the official to leave the property. He can block attempts to seize goods. He can stop actions based on statutory rules that do not reflect natural law. His authority to do this is lawful because natural law outranks statute. Statutes bind the fiction. Natural law binds the living.

The sheriff must understand the difference between a claim and a demand. A claim is lawful when it involves harm. A demand is lawful only when consent exists. Institutions issue demands routinely, even when consent is absent. These demands are directed at the fiction, not the living. A sheriff who understands this distinction protects the people from demands that have no lawful foundation. He teaches the community how to recognise the difference. This knowledge weakens the control that institutions attempt to assert.

A sheriff also protects the people from intimidation. Institutions often use intimidation when they cannot prove jurisdiction. They threaten enforcement. They threaten penalties. They threaten escalation. They rely on fear to create compliance. But fear has no place in natural law. Fear is a tool of control. Honour is a tool of justice. When the sheriff stands in honour, intimidation loses its power. Officials who expect immediate compliance become unsettled when the sheriff calmly requests proof of authority. They encounter a barrier that their training did not prepare them for. They cannot override natural law through force when the community stands behind their sheriff.

Another core duty of the sheriff is to uphold the decisions of the common law court. When a common law court reaches a judgment, the sheriff ensures that the remedy is carried out peacefully and fairly. He does not punish. He does not coerce. He simply ensures that the agreed remedy is honoured. This reinforces the authority of the court. It shows that the people stand behind their decisions. It demonstrates that natural law is stronger than statutory force.

This responsibility requires the sheriff to be steady and principled. He must treat both sides of a dispute with fairness. He must ensure that the remedy is proportionate to the harm. He must ensure that no one is treated with cruelty or disrespect. His role is to protect peace, not create conflict. A sheriff who behaves aggressively breaks the principles of natural law. A sheriff who behaves calmly strengthens the legitimacy of the court.

A sheriff may also be called to serve notices on behalf of the people. Notice is a core concept within natural law. A man cannot be held accountable for something he does not know. A woman cannot be expected to respond to claims she has not received. Notice must be delivered by a living soul, not by an institution acting through automated systems. When a sheriff delivers notice, he does so with clarity and transparency. He ensures that the individual receiving it understands the content. He speaks openly and respectfully. This direct interaction prevents misunderstanding and supports fairness.

A sheriff must also understand trespass. Trespass is one of the most fundamental violations under natural law. It involves crossing boundaries without consent. Trespass can be physical, verbal, or administrative. Institutions often trespass administratively. They issue demands without lawful cause. They act without consent. They assume authority over the living. A common law sheriff recognises administrative trespass and protects the people from it. He reminds officials that authority must be proven, not assumed. He stands as the barrier between unlawful interference and the rights of the people.

A sheriff must remain neutral in all matters. His authority comes from the community, not from personal alliances. If he favours one group over another, he betrays his oath. If he allows his judgment to be shaped by personal interest, he undermines the legitimacy of the court. Neutrality ensures fairness. Neutrality ensures respect. Neutrality ensures that the community trusts the sheriff as a protector, not a participant in disputes. This trust strengthens the court and stabilises the community.

The sheriff also has a preventive role. By simply existing, he reduces the likelihood of harm or fraud. People behave with greater honour when they know the community holds strong principles. Institutions behave more cautiously when they know the people understand natural law. The presence of a common law sheriff signals that the community is awake. It shows that the people recognise their authority. It warns institutions that their actions will be scrutinised. This preventive effect is one of the greatest strengths of the sheriff's role.

A sheriff must also understand remedy. Remedy is the heart of justice. The sheriff ensures that remedy is applied with fairness, not force. He helps individuals comply with remedies that require effort or cooperation. He supports communication between the parties. He encourages voluntary compliance. If someone resists, he approaches the situation calmly and respectfully, ensuring that the community stands behind the decision. This approach preserves peace and strengthens unity.

The sheriff is also responsible for teaching the community about natural law. Knowledge strengthens freedom. Confusion strengthens institutions. A sheriff who shares knowledge empowers the people. He helps them understand their rights. He helps them understand jurisdiction. He helps them understand consent. This knowledge protects them from unlawful interference. It allows them to stand with clarity. It inspires them to act with honour.

A common law sheriff becomes a symbol of living authority. He represents the idea that law belongs to the people. He represents the principle that natural rights outrank statutes. He represents the truth that honour cannot be replaced by procedure. His presence restores confidence in natural justice. It inspires communities to form their own courts. It strengthens the belief that the people have the power to govern themselves peacefully.

The sheriff's authority lasts only as long as the people recognise it. This ensures that he remains accountable. He cannot become corrupt. He cannot misuse his position. The people can remove him at any time. This ensures that the office remains pure. It ensures that the sheriff always acts with integrity. It ensures that natural law remains the guiding force behind every action he takes.

ELECTING A COMMON LAW SHERIFF

A common law sheriff does not appear through appointment. He does not receive his authority from an institution. He does not gain power through a contract, licence, or certificate. His authority comes only from the people. The election of a common law sheriff is a living expression of community sovereignty. It shows that the people recognise their own power. It shows that they trust one of their own to protect their natural rights. It shows that they refuse to surrender their safety to institutions that act without honour.

The process of electing a sheriff begins with the people acknowledging their need for a guardian of peace. Every community requires someone who stands firm when conflict arises, someone who speaks truthfully when others remain silent, someone who understands natural law so clearly that he can recognise lawful authority and reject unlawful interference. This recognition marks the starting point. The people understand that natural rights require protection, and they look among themselves for a man who embodies honour, fairness, and strength.

Before the election begins, the people gather in an assembly. The assembly is open. Every living member of the community may attend. The purpose of the gathering is to recognise the authority of the living and to ensure that the process reflects natural principles. No institution may oversee the election. No statutory officer may interfere. The assembly belongs to the people alone. This is essential because the sheriff must serve the people, not any external system.

The assembly begins with a declaration. The people declare openly that they are a community of living men and women standing in natural authority. This declaration is important because it sets the foundation for everything that follows. It shows that the people understand where lawful authority begins. It shows that the people understand the difference between natural law and statute. It shows that the people recognise that they, not institutions, are the rightful source of authority.

After the declaration, the assembly calls for nominations. Anyone may nominate a man for the role of sheriff. The nominee must be a living man who stands in honour. He must be someone who has shown integrity in his actions. He must be someone who has earned the respect of the community. He must be someone who understands natural law and is willing to protect it. The people know who these men are. They know who stands with truth and who does not. A community always recognises honour.

A nominee must accept the nomination freely. Consent is essential. A man cannot be forced into the role. Natural law requires that all lawful actions begin with consent. If a nominee accepts, he steps forward and speaks to the assembly. He does not make promises like a politician. He does not sell himself as a candidate. He speaks as a living soul. He states that he will stand for truth, protect the peace, uphold natural law, and act in honour. This is not a campaign. It is an expression of willingness to serve.

The assembly then questions the nominee. This questioning is not adversarial. It is a test of character. The people ask about his understanding of natural law. They ask how he views authority. They ask how he would handle disputes. They ask how he would respond to unlawful interference by institutions. These questions reveal the nominee's clarity of thought. They reveal his courage. They reveal his commitment to honour. A man who seeks power will falter. A man who seeks to serve will stand firm.

A nominee who answers with sincerity gains the respect of the people. Respect is the foundation of authority. The sheriff must be respected because his role requires trust. He must be someone who will not misuse his position. He must be someone who understands that his authority comes from the people and can be withdrawn at any time. He must be someone who values peace more than control. The people recognise these qualities instinctively.

When questioning is complete, the assembly moves to the vote. The vote is open and public. There are no secret ballots. Secret ballots belong to systems that fear transparency. In natural law, transparency strengthens trust. Each man and woman stands and declares their vote aloud. They do not hide their choice. They speak openly because the sheriff must be someone they trust with their safety and their rights. This openness keeps the process honest.

The nominee must receive clear support from the community. This support may come through consensus or majority, depending on the size of the assembly. What matters is that the sheriff is chosen by the people. His authority rests on their voice. Once chosen, he becomes the lawful guardian of their peace. This authority is not symbolic. It is not ceremonial. It is real because it is grounded in natural law and consent.

After the vote, the sheriff-elect takes his oath. The oath is the heart of the process. It is the point where the living soul accepts the duty placed upon him. He raises no hand to the state. He swears no allegiance to institutions. His oath is spoken before the people. He declares that he will protect the peace, uphold natural law, act without fear, and serve the community honestly. This oath binds him in honour. It is not a contract. It is a living commitment.

The people then acknowledge his oath. This acknowledgement completes the election. The sheriff's authority becomes active because the people have recognised it. Authority in natural law is circular. It flows from the people to the sheriff and back to the people. The sheriff does not stand above the community. He stands within it. His authority is a reflection of their collective strength.

Once elected, the sheriff must be properly recognised by the community. This recognition may include a written declaration signed by the assembly. This document is not a licence. It is not permission. It is a record of truth. It shows that the sheriff was chosen lawfully by the people. It may be used to demonstrate legitimacy to institutions that attempt to challenge the sheriff's authority.

After recognition, the sheriff's role begins immediately. His presence stabilises the community. People feel safer when they know they have a guardian who stands in natural law. Institutions become more cautious when they know the community does not recognise their assumptions of authority. The election of a sheriff sends a clear message. The people understand their rights. The people stand together. The people will not be intimidated.

A newly elected sheriff must begin by strengthening relationships within the community. He must speak with the people he serves. He must listen to their concerns. He must understand their disputes. He must learn the dynamics of the community. He must know who may need protection. A sheriff who understands his community can act effectively. A sheriff who is disconnected cannot.

He must also study natural law with depth. Natural law is simple, but simplicity requires clarity. He must understand that all lawful authority begins with harm, loss, or fraud. He must understand that consent defines jurisdiction. He must understand that institutions cannot override the rights of the living. He must understand the difference between lawful authority and statutory instruction. This knowledge strengthens him. It allows him to stand firmly when challenged.

The sheriff must also develop wisdom in communication. His power lies not in force, but in clarity. A sheriff who can speak calmly in the face of aggression carries great authority. A sheriff who can explain natural law to officials undermines their attempts to intimidate. A sheriff who can reassure a frightened member of the community strengthens unity. Communication rooted in honour becomes a powerful tool.

The people must also support their sheriff. A sheriff cannot act alone. He must have the backing of the community. When the community stands with him, institutions hesitate. They recognise that the sheriff represents collective authority. They recognise that the people understand natural law. They recognise that the old methods of control will not work. This collective support protects the sheriff and empowers the people.

Once a sheriff has been elected, the community must strengthen the foundation that supports his authority. A sheriff cannot stand alone. His authority flows from the living, and he must remain rooted in the people at every moment. For this reason the community continues to act as the guiding force. They do not step back after the election. They do not treat the sheriff as a separate power. They remain active participants in the exercise of natural law. This ongoing involvement ensures that the sheriff remains accountable, honourable, and effective.

The first responsibility of the community after electing their sheriff is to affirm the legitimacy of the process. Legitimacy under natural law comes from truth, transparency, and consent. The people must record the election in writing. This record is not created for institutions. It is created for the people themselves. It is evidence of their decision. It shows that they acted lawfully. It shows that the sheriff holds authority grounded in consent. This written record becomes a living document, not a corporate certificate, and it may be signed by those present to reaffirm their collective standing.

The sheriff must be introduced to the broader community, especially to those who may not have attended the assembly. Presence is important. Authority must be seen. The sheriff stands before the people and speaks openly. He states his oath again so that those who were not present understand his duty. He explains the principles of natural law. He speaks about honour. He speaks about peace. He speaks about the sacred responsibility placed upon him. This openness builds trust. It ensures that everyone understands the role he has accepted.

After this introduction the sheriff begins building relationships. A sheriff must be more than a symbol. He must be connected to the people he serves. He must know their concerns. He must understand the strengths and weaknesses of the community. This understanding cannot be created from a distance. It requires direct interaction. A sheriff meets with families. He listens to their challenges. He observes patterns of conflict. He identifies individuals who may require protection. His authority grows stronger when he understands the real lives of the people.

The sheriff must also prepare himself for challenges from statutory institutions. Institutions will attempt to question his authority. They will attempt to confuse him. They will attempt to intimidate him. They may even attempt to ignore him. This is because statutory systems rely on assumed authority, and the presence of a common law sheriff exposes the limits of that assumption. To remain effective the sheriff must understand the tools that institutions use. He must understand statutory language. He must understand how institutions rely on the legal fiction. He must understand how to stand firmly in natural law when confronted by those who depend on procedure.

A common law sheriff must learn to distinguish between lawful claims and unlawful demands. A lawful claim involves harm, loss, or fraud. An unlawful demand is based on regulation, policy, or assumed jurisdiction. Institutions often issue demands disguised as lawful authority. When a sheriff encounters such a demand, he examines it carefully. He asks for proof. He requests evidence of harm. He requires that the official identify a living soul who has suffered loss. When the institution cannot provide this, the sheriff exposes the demand as unlawful. This ability to separate lawful authority from unlawful interference is essential.

The sheriff also becomes the main point of contact when community members face intimidation. Many institutions use intimidation when their authority is questioned. They rely on fear. They rely on confusion. They rely on silence. A sheriff breaks these patterns. When a member of the community receives an unlawful notice or faces aggressive behaviour from an official, the sheriff stands with them. He speaks on their behalf if they struggle to express their position. He reminds the official of natural law. He asks the official to justify his actions. He protects the individual from being coerced into acting as the legal fiction.

Communication becomes one of the sheriff's strongest tools. A sheriff who speaks with confidence can dismantle the intimidation tactics used by institutions. He does not shout. He does not threaten. He does not escalate. His strength is calm. His strength is clarity. His strength is truth. When a sheriff calmly states that he represents the living and stands under natural law, institutions struggle to respond. Their authority depends on submission. They have no response when confronted with honour.

A sheriff must also understand the power of presence. Presence is not physical force. It is the projection of certainty. When a sheriff arrives at a situation, the people recognise that the living have authority. Officials recognise that they cannot proceed without proving their claims. Presence brings balance to situations that might otherwise escalate. A man acting alone may struggle to stand against unlawful interference. A man standing with his sheriff feels the strength of the entire community behind him.

The election of a sheriff also requires the community to develop a support structure. The sheriff cannot be everywhere at once. He may need deputies. Deputies are not statutory officers. They are trusted members of the community who understand natural law and assist the sheriff in maintaining peace. Deputies must be chosen with the same care as the sheriff himself. They must be honourable. They must be fair. They must be calm. Their role is to support, not dominate.

A common law sheriff must also be ready to support the common law court. When the people gather to form a court, the sheriff ensures that the process is protected. He prevents interference from institutions. He ensures that everyone present acts with respect. He ensures that the proceedings remain peaceful. His presence reinforces the authority of the court. It shows that the people have organised themselves and will not tolerate unlawful intrusion.

When a common law court reaches a decision, the sheriff assists in carrying out the remedy. He does not act as an enforcer. He acts as a guide. If the remedy requires a man to restore property, the sheriff ensures the process is fair. If the remedy requires a woman to apologise for harm caused, the sheriff ensures the apology is given in sincerity, not coercion. If the remedy requires the correction of fraud, the sheriff ensures that the truth is recorded. His involvement ensures that the remedy is carried out in honour.

A sheriff also becomes a teacher. Knowledge strengthens the people. Confusion weakens them. The sheriff educates the community about natural law, consent, and jurisdiction. He teaches them how to stand in honour. He teaches them how to respond when institutions attempt to trespass. He teaches them how to recognise unlawful authority. He teaches them how to support the common law court. This education lifts the entire community. It transforms fear into understanding. It transforms confusion into strength. It transforms dependence into sovereignty.

Another key responsibility of the sheriff is to help resolve conflicts within the community before they escalate into court matters. Courts exist to handle serious disputes, but many issues can be resolved peacefully with early intervention. The sheriff listens to both sides. He encourages dialogue. He reminds them of natural principles. He helps them find a path of honour. His involvement prevents unnecessary disputes and strengthens unity.

As the sheriff grows in his role, institutions will notice. They may attempt to challenge him openly. They may demand authority. They may threaten action. These attempts reveal their fear. Institutions fear common law sheriffs because they cannot control them. They cannot compel them. They cannot intimidate them. A sheriff grounded in natural law cannot be moved by threats. He speaks truthfully. He stands firmly. He acts with integrity. Institutions eventually recognise that they have no lawful claim over the living.

The sheriff must also remember that his authority is temporary. It lasts only as long as the people recognise it. This prevents corruption. It ensures that the sheriff remains humble. He cannot misuse his position because the people can remove him. This safeguard keeps the role pure. It keeps natural law at the centre of everything. It ensures that the community remains the true holder of authority.

Electing a sheriff is one of the greatest acts of sovereignty a community can perform. It shows that the people know their authority. It shows that they trust each other. It shows that they can organise without relying on institutions. It shows that they can protect themselves. It shows that natural law is alive. It shows that honour still guides the living.

JURISDICTION AND THE POWER OF CONSENT

Jurisdiction is the foundation upon which every claim of authority rests. Without jurisdiction, no court has power. Without jurisdiction, no officer holds authority. Without jurisdiction, no institution can make demands. Jurisdiction determines whether any action taken against a man or a woman is lawful or unlawful. Understanding jurisdiction means understanding the true balance of power between the living and the systems that attempt to rule them.

Jurisdiction in statutory courts is built on a single assumption, the assumption of consent. These courts do not begin with natural law. They do not begin with harm, loss, or fraud. They begin with the belief that the individual standing before them has agreed to be governed by statutory rules. This belief is rarely questioned because most people do not know they have the power to withhold consent. They assume statutory courts possess automatic authority. They assume the judge outranks them. They assume the building carries lawful force. These assumptions allow the system to operate.

In natural law jurisdiction is simple. A man has authority over himself. A woman has authority over herself. No one else can make lawful claims against them unless harm, loss, or fraud has occurred. Natural law does not recognise jurisdiction based on paperwork. It does not recognise jurisdiction based on titles. It does not recognise jurisdiction based on procedure. It recognises only one thing. Consent. If consent is absent, jurisdiction is absent. This truth restores power to the living.

Consent can be given openly or silently. Institutions rely on silent consent. When a man remains quiet, the statutory court assumes he agrees. When a woman answers to a name written on paper, the court assumes she accepts the role of the legal fiction. When people participate without questioning authority, the court assumes they have agreed to its jurisdiction. This is why statutory systems teach people to comply without thinking. They rely on habits that create silent consent.

Silent consent has no place in natural law. Natural law requires clarity. It requires understanding. It requires agreement. A man cannot be forced into contract. A woman cannot be obligated by confusion. A community cannot be governed by assumption. Consent must be expressed knowingly. It must be given freely. It must be made by the living, not the fiction. Once the people understand this, statutory authority weakens.

Statutory systems use specific methods to manufacture consent. They use language. They use titles. They use paperwork. They use intimidation. They use roles created for the legal fiction. When a man answers to the name on a document, he is assumed to be acting as the fiction. When a woman stands behind a corporate strawman, she becomes bound by statutory obligations. The court's power emerges not from law, but from participation. Participation becomes consent. Consent becomes jurisdiction.

A man who understands natural law does not give silent consent. He speaks clearly. He states that he is the living soul. He does not accept the role of the fiction. He does not stand under statutory authority. He requires the court to prove jurisdiction. This is where the system struggles. It cannot prove jurisdiction under natural law. It can only claim jurisdiction through statute. It can only rely on assumptions. It can only use intimidation and procedure. When a man refuses silent consent, the illusion begins to collapse.

Consent also shapes contracts. Statutes operate as commercial rules. They only apply when a man enters contract. A contract requires offer, acceptance, and consideration. If any of these elements are missing, no lawful contract exists. Statutory systems present statutes as if they were law, but they function as terms of agreement for the legal fiction. When the living refuse to act as the fiction, they step outside these agreements. Institutions know this, but they rely on confusion to bind the living into contracts they did not knowingly enter.

Natural law teaches that consent cannot be created through fear. A man who agrees under threat has not consented. A woman who agrees under coercion has not consented. A community that is pressured has not given lawful authority. Statutory systems violate this principle routinely. They issue threats. They warn of penalties. They use fear to push people into agreements. A sheriff who stands in natural law recognises these tactics. He prevents institutions from manufacturing consent through intimidation.

Jurisdiction can also be challenged openly. A man may ask a simple question, what authority do you claim over me? A statutory officer will often respond with titles, codes, or regulations. None of these prove jurisdiction. A title is a role. A code is a rule for the fiction. A regulation is an instruction for administrative entities. A natural man is not bound by these unless he consents. When the officer cannot answer the question, his authority collapses. This collapse reveals the truth. The living outrank statutory roles.

Courts rely on a similar illusion. A judge expects the people to believe that his position gives him automatic authority. Yet his authority exists only through the consent of those who stand before him. When a man asserts his natural standing, the judge must prove jurisdiction. The judge cannot. Judges rely on participation. They rely on titles such as defendant or claimant. They rely on the living stepping into roles created for the fiction. When those roles are rejected, the judge loses commercial jurisdiction.

Consent also determines whether statutory penalties apply. Penalties issued without harm, loss, or fraud are administrative. They apply only to the fiction. When a man pays a penalty, he accepts responsibility for the fiction. When he refuses and stands as the living, the penalty loses force. This is why institutions pressure people to act quickly. They want the fiction validated before the man realises the truth. They want acceptance before the woman asserts her standing. Once acceptance occurs, the contract becomes active.

Natural law offers clarity. A man is accountable only for harm he has caused. A woman is accountable only for loss she has created. A community is accountable only for fraud it has committed. No statute overrides this. No code replaces this. No underlined policy can change this. When institutions attempt to assert authority without natural justification, they trespass. Trespass under natural law is unlawful interference. A sheriff protects individuals from this interference by requiring institutions to prove jurisdiction. When they cannot, their claim ends.

Consent also plays a role in community governance. A community that stands together under natural law forms its own jurisdiction. This jurisdiction exists through collective consent. It does not need approval from the state. It does not need recognition from institutions. It exists because the people recognise each other. It exists because the people uphold honour. It exists because the people agree to resolve disputes peacefully. This jurisdiction is lawful because it is grounded in the natural rights of the living.

A common law court operates within this natural jurisdiction. When the people gather, they create lawful authority. When they form a jury, they activate natural judgment. When they reach a decision, they express lawful remedy. The court's jurisdiction does not come from statute. It comes from consent. The people consent to be heard. They consent to hear others. They consent to uphold honour. This consent creates lawful jurisdiction that no institution can override.

Understanding the power of consent allows the people to reclaim authority. They no longer fear institutions. They no longer submit automatically. They no longer accept assumed authority. They stand as the living. They speak clearly. They ask questions. They reject roles that do not apply. They refuse silent consent. This change transforms the balance of power. Institutions lose strength when the people refuse to submit.

Consent is the point where authority begins and ends. Institutions rely on the public never understanding this. They want people to believe authority flows from government to the people. Natural law teaches the opposite. Authority flows from the people to any structure they choose to recognise. Once this truth is understood, the definition of jurisdiction becomes clear. Jurisdiction is nothing more than the space in which an individual or a community has agreed to be bound. When consent is withdrawn, that space dissolves.

This truth becomes visible when you observe how statutory courts behave when jurisdiction is questioned. A man who asks the judge to prove jurisdiction does not receive a lawful answer. He is told vague phrases about the court having inherent authority. He is told that jurisdiction is obvious. He is told that questioning it is inappropriate. He is told that the matter will proceed regardless. These responses are not proof. They are avoidance. They reveal the weakness of statutory authority. If the judge held true jurisdiction, he would prove it without hesitation.

The judge cannot prove jurisdiction because statutory authority does not reach the living automatically. It reaches the legal fiction. It reaches the corporate entity created on paper. It reaches the name written in capital letters. When the living man refuses to step into the role of that fiction, the court's foundation collapses. This collapse does not happen through rebellion. It happens through clarity. It happens through the withdrawal of consent. It happens when the man states openly that he stands under natural law and does not accept statutory jurisdiction.

Institutions fear this clarity because their authority depends on confusion. They attempt to mix the roles of the living and the fiction. They speak as if the two are the same. They write notices addressed to the fiction but treat them as obligations for the living. They rely on people never noticing the separation. They assume that the public will continue to act as surety for the fiction. They assume that the fear of penalties will override the desire to understand natural law. These assumptions hold their system together.

A community that understands consent breaks these assumptions. When individuals refuse to act as the fiction, institutions must face the living directly. When institutions face the living, they must prove jurisdiction. They cannot. This is why natural law is powerful. It does not require force. It requires recognition. When people recognise the truth, they cannot be controlled in the same way. Consent is withdrawn silently, calmly, and lawfully.

Withdrawal of consent must be expressed clearly. Silence is not enough because statutory systems interpret silence as agreement. A man who does not speak becomes a participant by default. A woman who does not challenge assumptions becomes bound through procedure. Withdrawal must be expressed in words. It must be stated directly. It must be spoken as the living. Once expressed, it removes the foundation upon which statutory authority rests.

Consent may also be conditional. Conditional consent is one of the most powerful tools within natural law. A man may say, I conditionally accept your claim upon proof of jurisdiction. A woman may say, I conditionally accept your demand upon evidence of authority. Conditional acceptance places the burden on the institution. It requires them to demonstrate lawful standing. They cannot rely on assumptions. They cannot hide behind procedure. They must prove their claim. When they fail to provide proof, their claim dissolves lawfully. This method protects the living without conflict.

Institutions fear conditional acceptance because it exposes their lack of jurisdiction. They respond with threats. They respond with warnings. They respond with symbolic authority. None of this replaces lawful proof. The more they escalate, the more obvious their lack of natural authority becomes. This weakness is visible to anyone who stands in truth.

Jurisdiction also depends on location. Statutory courts operate within their own commercial jurisdiction. That jurisdiction exists in buildings controlled by the state. Once inside, the people assume they have entered a lawful venue. They do not realise they have entered a corporate venue. A common law court can exist anywhere because it is created by the living. It does not require a special location. It does not require official furniture. It does not require the approval of institutions. It exists wherever the people choose to stand together.

A man who understands jurisdiction may question the authority of a statutory court by asking, what is the nature and cause of this court? If the court is a statutory venue, it cannot claim to be a court of natural law. It cannot claim to serve the living. It must admit, either directly or through its behaviour, that it serves statutory regulations. These regulations apply only to the legal fiction unless the living consents. Once this is understood, the man knows he is not bound automatically by their rules.

Jurisdiction also requires proper service of notice. A notice must be delivered lawfully. It must be addressed to the correct party. A notice addressed to the fiction does not bind the living. Institutions rely on the fact that the living respond anyway. They create the jurisdiction by participating. A man who understands natural law rejects notices addressed to the fiction. He states that the fiction is not present. He does not accept responsibility for it. By doing this, he prevents the court from assuming jurisdiction.

Consent is also linked to understanding. A man cannot consent to something he does not understand. A woman cannot be bound by words she does not comprehend. A community cannot accept obligations hidden within complex documents. Statutory systems rely on complexity to disguise the nature of consent. They use technical language. They use references to other statutes. They use terms defined differently in legal dictionaries. These tactics obscure the truth. They hide the fact that many statutory obligations function as contracts.

Natural law requires transparency. A contract must be clear. Agreement must be informed. Anything less is deception. Deception invalidates consent. A court that relies on hidden meaning does not act in honour. A government that hides obligations within statutes does not operate lawfully. A system that manipulates through complexity violates natural law. A common law court rejects all such tactics. It relies on direct communication. It relies on clarity. It relies on truth.

Consent also creates community jurisdiction. When a group of living men and women agree to stand together under natural law, they create lawful authority. This authority is not symbolic. It is real. It is binding. It creates a space where natural law governs every action. This jurisdiction cannot be overridden by statutory systems. It cannot be revoked by institutions. It cannot be dismissed by corporate courts. It exists because the people exist.

A common law court is the expression of this jurisdiction. When the people gather, they activate their natural authority. When they form a jury, they exercise it. When they reach a decision, they express it. When the sheriff enforces remedy, he protects it. This jurisdiction is lawful because it reflects consent, honour, fairness, and truth. No institution can claim higher authority than the living. Institutions can only operate with consent. Once the people withdraw consent, institutions lose power.

Consent is therefore both shield and sword. It protects the people from unlawful claims. It empowers the people to create lawful authority. It dissolves statutory jurisdiction when withdrawn. It strengthens common law jurisdiction when expressed. It is the central force that defines all lawful interactions.

A community that understands consent cannot be controlled by assumed authority. Institutions cannot manipulate them. Courts cannot intimidate them. Officials cannot trespass against them. The people stand as the source of authority. They choose their own processes. They resolve their own disputes. They protect their own peace.

RUNNING HEARINGS IN A COMMON LAW COURT

A hearing in a common law court is the purest expression of natural justice. It is the moment when the people come together to listen, to question, and to reach truth. Unlike statutory courts, which rely on rigid procedure, commercial paperwork, and roles created for the fiction, a common law hearing is shaped by honour, clarity, and direct communication. The process is simple because justice is simple. When the people listen with sincerity, truth reveals itself. When the people act with fairness, justice follows naturally.

A hearing begins with the assembly. The assembly is made up of living men and women who consent to participate in the process. Consent is essential. No one can be compelled to take part. A common law court holds no authority over someone who refuses to stand within its jurisdiction. Jurisdiction comes from consent, and consent comes from the living. When the assembly gathers in full awareness of their natural authority, they create a lawful environment where truth can be spoken freely.

Before any hearing begins, the foreman confirms that everyone present understands their role. The foreman does not act as a judge. He does not sit above the people. He does not possess special powers. His role is to guide the proceedings, keep discussion orderly, and ensure fairness. He reminds the assembly that they serve truth, not opinion. He reminds the speakers that they must act in honour. He reminds everyone that harm, loss, and fraud are the only true violations under natural law.

The hearing then begins with a clear statement of the matter. The foreman describes the dispute in plain language. This statement is not a charge. It is not an accusation written in statutory terms. It is a simple description of what has occurred and why the matter has been brought before the people. This clarity ensures that everyone understands the purpose of the hearing. There is no confusion. There are no hidden claims. Everything is open.

The parties involved speak as living souls. They are not called defendants or claimants. These statutory labels do not apply in natural law. They confuse the process by creating artificial roles. The living speak for themselves. The man who brings the claim speaks first. He describes what happened. He explains how harm was caused. He shows evidence of loss. He identifies any deception that occurred. His words must be honest. His behaviour must reflect honour. If he speaks falsely, the people will recognise it immediately.

After he speaks, the man or woman responding to the claim has the opportunity to answer. They do not need representation. They do not need legal counsel. They do not need scripted language. They speak plainly, directly, and truthfully. They describe their side of the matter. They present their evidence. They respond to the allegations. They may admit wrongdoing. They may dispute the claim. They may provide context. Their voice is heard, and the assembly listens without prejudice.

In a common law hearing, the people weigh the words of both parties through conscience. Conscience is the highest court. It recognises sincerity. It recognises deception. It recognises fear, anger, confusion, and truth. Statutory courts dismiss conscience as irrelevant. They replace it with procedure. Yet conscience is the clearest guide to justice because it is rooted in natural law. Every participant brings their conscience into the hearing, and together these consciences form a powerful vessel for truth.

Evidence is considered openly. There is no hidden process. There are no secret submissions. Every piece of evidence is shared with the assembly. Evidence may include spoken testimony, written statements, physical items, or witness accounts. The people decide what carries weight. They decide what reflects truth. They decide what reveals deception. Unlike statutory courts, which impose strict rules about what evidence may be considered, a common law court accepts all evidence that helps uncover the truth.

Witnesses play a crucial role in the hearing. A witness is any living soul who has information relevant to the matter. Witnesses speak freely. They take an oath to speak truthfully. This oath is not ceremonial. It binds the witness in honour. A man who lies in a common law court damages his reputation. A woman who lies brings dishonour upon herself. The community will know, and this knowledge carries real consequences. Statutory systems punish perjury through penalties. Common law systems enforce truthfulness through honour, which is far more meaningful.

The jury listens throughout the hearing. The jurors do not act as passive observers. They ask questions when clarity is needed. They request additional information if something is unclear. They speak respectfully, but they engage actively. Their duty is to understand the matter fully before reaching a conclusion. They do not rely on lawyers or judges to interpret facts. They rely on direct truth spoken by the living. This direct interaction strengthens the legitimacy of the process.

During the hearing the foreman ensures that the process remains balanced. He prevents interruptions. He prevents hostility. He prevents personal attacks. He reminds the assembly that their purpose is to restore peace, not escalate conflict. If emotions run high, he pauses the hearing and reminds everyone of their duty to act in honour. This steady guidance prevents disputes from spiralling into chaos. It keeps the focus on truth.

One of the most important features of a common law hearing is the absence of legal jargon. Legal jargon is used by statutory systems to create confusion. It separates the people from their own authority. It hides meaning behind technical terms. A common law court rejects such language. Everyone speaks in simple, clear, direct words. This simplicity ensures fairness. It ensures understanding. It ensures that justice is accessible.

Another defining feature is transparency. Statutory systems hide much of the process behind closed doors. Judges meet in chambers. Legal representatives negotiate privately. Documents move unseen. This secrecy undermines trust. A common law hearing is the opposite. Everything is visible. Everything is heard. Everything is recorded. Transparency protects the people from manipulation. It prevents corruption. It ensures that justice is not controlled by a small group.

After the parties have spoken and the evidence has been presented, the hearing enters the period of questioning. The jurors ask questions. The assembly may ask questions through the foreman. The purpose of questioning is not to interrogate. It is to seek clarity. It is to understand why the dispute occurred. It is to uncover the intent behind actions. Intent matters because natural law recognises that harm done knowingly differs from harm done accidentally. Statutory systems overlook this. A common law court investigates it deeply.

The hearing then shifts into deliberation. The jury discusses the matter openly. They do not retreat into secrecy. They speak where the people can hear them. They express their thoughts with honesty. They consider the evidence carefully. They consider the behaviour of the parties. They consider the principles of natural law. They ask themselves whether harm occurred. They ask themselves whether loss was suffered. They ask themselves whether fraud took place. These questions guide them toward a conclusion.

During deliberation, the assembly listens. The assembly ensures fairness. If a juror begins to act with bias, the assembly corrects him. If a juror becomes confused, the assembly offers clarity. This collective oversight keeps the process grounded in truth. Deliberation ends when the jurors reach agreement. Agreement does not require perfection. It requires sincerity. It requires fairness. It requires recognition of truth.

When the jury is ready, the foreman announces that a conclusion has been reached. The announcement is made clearly and openly. The people listen. The parties listen. This announcement does not represent the personal opinion of the foreman. It reflects the collective judgment of the jury acting through natural law. The authority behind the announcement comes from the living, not from institutions. The people recognise this authority because they participated in the process.

When the jury reaches its conclusion, the foreman prepares to speak it aloud. This moment is not ceremonial. It is the living expression of community judgment. It is the point where truth becomes remedy. It is the moment when natural law is activated through the people. In a statutory court the decision belongs to a judge who sits above the people. In a common law court the decision belongs to the people themselves. This distinction reveals the true difference between the two systems. One controls. The other restores.

The foreman rises and addresses the assembly. He speaks clearly. He states the facts as they were found. He states whether harm, loss, or fraud occurred. He declares the remedy required to restore balance. His words carry authority because they reflect the judgment of the jury, not the dictates of a statute. Natural law flows through the people, and the foreman becomes the voice of that law for a brief moment. This voice is powerful because it is grounded in truth, not procedure.

Once the decision is announced, the parties involved have the opportunity to respond. They may accept the decision. They may ask for clarification. They may express concerns. This is not an appeal in the statutory sense. It is a continuation of the honour-based process. If a party speaks in honesty, the assembly listens. If someone raises an issue that the jury overlooked, the jury may choose to consider it. The process remains flexible because justice must reflect fairness, not rigidity. A natural law system adapts to truth. A statutory system forces truth into its own structure.

The remedy becomes the central focus. The purpose of remedy is to restore peace. Peace is the natural state of a community governed by honour. When harm is repaired, peace returns. When loss is restored, peace returns. When fraud is exposed and corrected, peace returns. Remedy may require repayment. It may require an apology. It may require the return of property. It may require service to the community. It may require a correction of record. What matters is not the form of remedy but the restoration it brings. The remedy must reflect the nature of the harm. It must be proportionate. It must be fair.

In a common law court remedy is personal. It involves the living. A man who caused harm must face the one he harmed. A woman who caused loss must restore it directly. The process does not hide behind third parties. It does not pass responsibility to institutions. It does not allow wrongdoers to escape accountability through technicalities. Statutory courts often treat penalties as debts owed to the state. Common law courts treat remedy as responsibility owed to the injured party. This directness strengthens justice.

Once the remedy is agreed, the sheriff becomes involved. His role is not to enforce through intimidation. His role is to ensure that the remedy is carried out peacefully. He stands as a witness. He stands as the guardian of fairness. He ensures that the responsible party completes the remedy. He ensures that the injured party receives restoration. He ensures that no one acts outside honour. The sheriff's presence strengthens the process because he represents the authority of the people standing behind their judgment.

The sheriff does not act alone. The community stands with him. The people recognise their own decision and expect it to be fulfilled. Community support creates a sense of responsibility. The responsible party understands that the entire community expects honourable completion of the remedy. This expectation encourages cooperation. It prevents evasion. It creates unity. When the community stands together, the process works naturally.

Remedy must be completed in a reasonable time. Natural law does not rush. It does not impose unrealistic deadlines. It requires sincerity. It requires genuine effort. If the remedy involves repayment, the sheriff ensures that the repayment schedule is fair to both sides. If the remedy involves labour or restoration, the sheriff ensures that it is carried out safely and without exploitation. If the remedy involves an apology, he ensures that it is given truthfully and respectfully. Each remedy reflects the nature of the dispute and the needs of the people involved.

A common law court also allows for continuing dialogue after remedy is delivered. The community may follow up with both parties. They may ensure that peace has truly returned. They may support individuals who struggled through the process. This follow up ensures that the effects of the hearing extend beyond the moment of decision. It strengthens bonds. It reduces future conflict. It reinforces the idea that justice is not a transaction. It is a living process.

One of the greatest strengths of a common law hearing is that every participant understands their role. There is no confusion. The people know why they are present. The foreman knows his duty. The jury knows their responsibility. The sheriff knows his purpose. The parties know their rights. This clarity ensures that justice is carried out in honour. Confusion is a weapon of statutory systems. Clarity is the foundation of natural law.

A hearing under natural law also teaches valuable lessons. It teaches the people the importance of standing in truth. It teaches them the value of listening. It teaches them how to recognise deception. It teaches them how to support each other. Each hearing strengthens the community. Each hearing reinforces natural principles. Each hearing prepares the people to resolve future disputes without fear or confusion.

A common law hearing also protects the dignity of the living. Statutory courts strip dignity away. They reduce people to case numbers. They force them into roles. They silence their voices. They treat them as objects within a commercial system. A common law court restores dignity by treating every participant as a living soul. Their words matter. Their truth matters. Their presence matters. This recognition of dignity is what makes natural justice superior to statutory procedure.

The absence of hierarchy in the hearing prevents corruption. No one holds absolute authority. Power is shared. Responsibility is shared. Truth is shared. The process cannot be hijacked by individuals seeking control. This structure ensures that justice remains pure. It prevents the emergence of elites who manipulate outcomes. It protects the people from domination. It maintains balance.

Another important feature of a common law hearing is that it cannot be used for malicious purposes. In statutory courts individuals can weaponise the system. They can file claims to cause financial harm. They can use procedure to punish innocent people. They can abuse the system. In a common law court the community prevents such abuse. The people recognise dishonour. A man who brings a false claim will be challenged. A woman who acts maliciously will be exposed. The community rejects dishonour openly. This protection ensures that the court remains a place of truth, not revenge.

The hearing strengthens the role of the sheriff. As he observes the process he sees the dynamics of the community. He sees where conflict arises. He sees who may require guidance. He sees who may struggle to express themselves. He sees who may be vulnerable. This understanding helps him fulfil his role. It allows him to protect more effectively. It allows him to intervene early when disputes emerge. It allows him to strengthen peace before harm occurs.

A common law hearing is not a performance. It is not a ritual. It is not a symbolic exercise. It is the real application of law by the people who live under it. It is the living expression of sovereignty. It is the demonstration of the people's authority to resolve disputes without surrendering control to institutions. When the people run hearings themselves, they reclaim justice. They bring it back to its natural home.

The conclusion of a hearing is not an ending. It is the beginning of restored relationships. It is the beginning of renewed trust. It is the beginning of a stronger community standing in natural law. It shows that the people are capable of resolving disputes without the need for statutory systems. It shows that justice is alive. It shows that honour guides the living.

COMMON LAW ENFORCEMENT

Common law enforcement is not the enforcement of power. It is the protection of peace. It does not rely on force, threat, or intimidation. It does not act through statutory authority, commercial penalty, or administrative punishment. It acts through honour. It acts through truth. It acts through the natural authority of the living. When a community chooses to stand under common law, enforcement becomes a shared responsibility rooted in collective integrity rather than institutional control.

In statutory systems enforcement is the arm of power. Officers enforce codes. Bailiffs enforce debts. Inspectors enforce regulations. These roles exist to protect institutions, not the people. Their purpose is compliance. Their methods are pressure and fear. Their authority comes from statutes, not from natural law. This structure creates a force that stands above the people, claiming superiority based on written rules that do not reflect natural principles.

Common law enforcement reverses this structure. Authority does not rise above the people. Authority rises from the people. It is distributed. It is understood. It is accepted. The sheriff, the deputies, and the community all share responsibility. Enforcement is not a tool to dominate. It is a tool to maintain balance. Its purpose is not to punish wrongdoing. Its purpose is to ensure remedy, protect rights, and prevent further harm. This makes it fundamentally different from statutory enforcement.

The cornerstone of common law enforcement is consent. The people consent to uphold natural principles. They consent to support the sheriff. They consent to abide by remedy once a judgment is reached. Consent makes enforcement peaceful. When people understand natural law and agree to live by it, enforcement becomes unnecessary in many cases. Disputes resolve themselves because honour becomes the guiding force. Enforcement appears only when someone acts outside honour and refuses to repair harm.

A common law sheriff plays a central role. His authority is not derived from badges or uniforms. It comes from the trust placed in him by the community. He is the protector of peace. He ensures that decisions made by the common law court are carried out. He ensures that remedy agreed by the people is honoured. He intervenes when unlawful interference threatens someone's natural rights. Yet he is never an enforcer in the statutory sense. He is a guardian, not a controller.

When the sheriff must enforce a remedy, he does so through clarity. He reminds the responsible party why the remedy exists. He explains the harm that requires restoration. He speaks calmly. He does not threaten. He does not demand compliance through fear. He acts with the authority of natural law, which is grounded in truth. People respond differently to truth than to statutory commands. They recognise its legitimacy. They sense its fairness. They understand its purpose. This recognition makes compliance peaceful rather than forced.

If a responsible party refuses to honour a remedy, the sheriff does not escalate with force. He approaches with honour. He reminds the individual that refusal breaks peace. He explains that dishonour harms the community. He states that the people have recognised harm and agreed upon the remedy. He affirms that ignoring this agreement damages unity. Common law enforcement works because it depends on the conscience of the living. A man may resist statutory authority out of frustration or fear. He rarely resists the collective judgment of his own community.

The sheriff is supported by deputies. Deputies are not created through appointment by institutions. They are chosen by the people. They assist the sheriff only when necessary. Their role is to maintain peace during enforcement. They stand as witnesses. They ensure that actions remain honourable. They ensure that no aggression arises. Their presence discourages dishonour. They do not act with force. They act with authority granted by the people's consent.

If enforcement requires the recovery of property, the sheriff proceeds carefully. He does not seize property arbitrarily. He ensures that the property being recovered truly belongs to the injured party. He ensures that the removal of property does not escalate into hostility. He ensures that everyone involved understands the basis of the remedy. He ensures that no unnecessary harm occurs. In statutory systems property seizure often creates conflict because it is carried out by strangers acting under commercial rules. In common law enforcement the process is personal, accountable, and grounded in fairness.

Common law enforcement also applies to the protection of rights. If an institution attempts to trespass against a member of the community, the sheriff intervenes. Trespass may take many forms. It may be physical. It may be administrative. It may be verbal. It may be commercial. The sheriff's duty is to identify unlawful trespass based on natural principles. If no harm, loss, or fraud exists, the institution has no authority. The sheriff states this clearly. He instructs the official to cease interference. He prevents unlawful escalation. He defends the living from assumed authority.

Institutions often react with confusion when confronted by a common law sheriff. They expect compliance. They rely on fear. They assume that titles give them power. They are unprepared for someone who questions authority based on natural law. They may demand legal justification. They may repeat statutory language. They may threaten consequences. Yet none of this replaces the requirement for lawful authority. When the sheriff calmly asks for proof of harm, their claims collapse. Institutions cannot demonstrate harm because statutory enforcement is not based on natural law.

A sheriff must understand how to respond to escalation attempts. Institutions may attempt to summon statutory officers. They may attempt to involve police who act under codes rather than natural law. A sheriff stands firm. He speaks with clarity. He explains that jurisdiction has not been established. He states that the matter involves the living and is governed by natural law. Many statutory officers become uncertain because they recognise the limits of their authority. They may attempt to assert power through intimidation, yet intimidation loses force when confronted by calm, reasoned truth.

In unusual cases where an institution persists, the sheriff may gather the community. The presence of the people reinforces natural authority. It shows that the sheriff does not act alone. It shows that the community recognises unlawful trespass. It shows that the people will not permit institutions to override their rights. This collective presence often prevents further escalation. Institutions are reluctant to act aggressively in the face of unified resistance grounded in natural law.

Common law enforcement does not rely on punishment. Punishment belongs to statutory systems that seek control rather than justice. Punishment breeds resentment. Punishment creates cycles of harm. Punishment establishes dominance. Natural law does not recognise punishment as a remedy. It recognises restoration. When restoration is achieved, enforcement ends. The goal is to repair, not to ruin. The sheriff understands this. He never seeks to break a man. He seeks to restore balance.

If a dispute continues after remedy, the sheriff may assist the parties in further dialogue. He encourages them to speak openly. He helps them address unresolved issues. He ensures that the dispute does not reignite into harm. He acts as a stabilising force. This approach prevents small disputes from becoming larger conflicts. It strengthens the community through resolution rather than suppression.

Common law enforcement also protects the community from external threats. External threats may come from institutions, corporations, or individuals who attempt to impose authority through deception. The sheriff recognises these threats because he understands the difference between lawful authority and assumed power. He educates the community. He shows them how to identify trespass. He teaches them how to assert their rights. This education is enforcement in its highest form. It prevents harm before it occurs.

A sheriff who understands the principles of consent and jurisdiction can dismantle unlawful claims with a few words. He asks simple questions. Who is the injured party? Where is the evidence of harm? What authority do you claim over the living? These questions reveal assumptions. They expose deception. They place the burden of proof on the institution. This burden cannot be met, because statutory authority does not extend to the living without consent.

The community must support the sheriff for enforcement to remain lawful and peaceful. Their support gives him strength. Their unity protects him from retaliation. Their understanding of natural law reinforces his authority. When the people stand behind their sheriff, institutions recognise that their usual tactics will fail. This recognition creates a new balance of power. The people become the authority. The sheriff becomes the guardian. Institutions become secondary.

Common law enforcement continues only as long as honour requires it. The goal is always restoration. Once peace is restored, enforcement becomes unnecessary. This approach protects the dignity of the living. It prevents the growth of oppressive power structures. It ensures that authority remains with the people. Statutory systems do the opposite. They create ongoing punishment. They trap people in cycles of penalties. They create roles for enforcers and roles for offenders. These roles feed the system. Common law refuses these cycles. It ends conflict once balance is restored.

A sheriff enforcing natural law must understand that his authority is moral, not mechanical. Statutory officers rely on procedure. They point to documents. They follow policy. They take action because a system tells them to. A common law sheriff acts because truth requires it. He acts because the community recognises harm. He acts because remedy is needed. He never hides behind paperwork. He does not claim power through titles. His authority is recognised only when he behaves with integrity.

When a dispute continues after remedy is issued, the sheriff may call upon the assembly. The assembly becomes the balancing force. They listen again. They assess whether the remedy has been completed. They may decide that further action is required. They may decide that the dispute has been resolved and that one party is seeking additional advantage. Their judgment is final because the people themselves hold the authority. This ensures that enforcement does not become a tool for revenge. It remains a tool for peace.

A sheriff must be patient. Natural law does not hurry. It does not rush decisions. It does not force immediate compliance. It allows time for understanding. It allows time for healing. A man who caused harm may feel shame. This shame can make him defensive. When given time, he may come to accept responsibility. A sheriff who understands human nature allows this space. He recognises that true restoration often takes time. He guides the process without applying pressure.

Enforcement becomes more complex when institutions attempt to interfere. Institutions do not recognise the authority of natural law unless the people assert it firmly. When an institution sends officials to enforce statutory claims, the sheriff must stand between the official and the individual. He asks for proof of jurisdiction. He asks for evidence of harm. He asks for lawful authority. These questions disrupt the assumptions that institutions rely on. They force the official to confront the limits of his training.

A statutory officer may attempt to respond with codes or regulations. The sheriff listens politely. He then explains that codes apply only to the fiction, not the living. He states that the living do not stand under statutory jurisdiction without consent. He requires the official to identify the injured party. He does not allow the conversation to drift into confusion. He stays within natural law. This clarity creates uncertainty in the official. He expected compliance, not calm questioning. He expected submission, not knowledge.

The sheriff must also be prepared for situations where statutory officers attempt to use intimidation. Intimidation may be verbal or physical. A statutory officer may raise his voice. He may make threats. He may demand immediate compliance. None of this affects natural law. Intimidation does not create jurisdiction. Threats do not create authority. Noise does not create legitimacy. A sheriff trained in natural law responds with calm strength. He does not escalate. He does not retreat. He stands in truth.

If a situation continues to escalate, the sheriff may call for members of the community. Their presence changes everything. Statutory officers rely on the isolation of individuals. When they see a unified group standing behind their sheriff, they become cautious. They recognise that they cannot impose assumed authority on a community that knows its rights. They understand that they have no lawful foundation for acting against the living. This recognition often dissolves the conflict.

Common law enforcement also extends to protection from fraud. Fraud is one of the most damaging forms of harm because it often hides behind official language. Institutions use letters, notices, and demands that appear lawful but carry no natural authority. A sheriff must understand how to identify administrative fraud. Administrative fraud occurs when an institution makes a claim without natural justification. It may occur when an institution demands payment without a contract. It may occur when an institution issues a threat without jurisdiction. It may occur when an institution sends a notice addressed to the fiction but tries to apply it to the living.

The sheriff teaches the people how to recognise such fraud. He shows them how to read notices carefully. He shows them how to identify claims that rely on assumption. He shows them how to respond with conditional acceptance. Conditional acceptance protects the living. It forces the institution to prove authority. Institutions cannot provide such proof. This exposes the fraud. When fraud is exposed, the community becomes stronger.

Common law enforcement is also preventive. Prevention is not a concept recognised in statutory enforcement, which reacts only after harm occurs. A sheriff focused on natural law acts before harm grows. When he sees tensions rising between individuals, he speaks with them. He encourages dialogue. He reminds them of honour. He explains the importance of resolving disputes early. This simple intervention can prevent future conflict. It strengthens peace proactively. Natural law values prevention because it protects harmony.

The sheriff also acts as a guardian of community boundaries. Boundaries are essential. They protect the living from trespass. They protect property from unlawful interference. They protect families from unwanted intrusion. A sheriff teaches the people how to defend their boundaries lawfully. He explains that no official may step onto private land without consent. He explains that no institution may make demands without jurisdiction. He explains that the living must be approached with honour. These teachings prevent future violations.

Enforcement under natural law includes education. Education empowers the people. A sheriff holds gatherings to explain natural rights. He teaches the principles of harm, loss, and fraud. He teaches consent. He teaches jurisdiction. He teaches people how to speak clearly when challenged. He teaches them how to avoid silent consent. This education is enforcement because knowledge protects the community. Knowledge prevents harm. Knowledge strengthens sovereignty.

The sheriff may also engage with outside communities. When another group experiences interference from institutions, he may attend their gatherings to speak about natural law. This sharing of knowledge spreads strength. It builds alliances. It connects communities under common principles. It demonstrates that natural law is universal. It does not belong to one group. It belongs to all living souls. This unity strengthens the wider movement for sovereignty.

Common law enforcement requires consistency. The sheriff must act in honour consistently. He cannot act with honour one day and act with aggression the next. He cannot stand in truth only when convenient. People recognise inconsistency. They lose trust when honour wavers. The sheriff must hold himself to the highest standard. His behaviour becomes an example for the community. When he stands firmly, the people follow. When he falters, the community weakens.

Natural law enforcement also requires humility. A sheriff who becomes arrogant loses honour. A sheriff who believes he outranks the people forgets his purpose. A sheriff who seeks personal power undermines natural law. Humility ensures that the sheriff remains grounded. He serves, not rules. He protects, not dominates. He upholds natural law, not personal ambition. This humility ensures that the community continues to support him.

When enforcement is complete, the sheriff reports to the assembly. He describes the actions taken. He explains how the remedy was carried out. He shares any concerns. This transparency keeps the community informed. It prevents misunderstanding. It maintains trust. Statutory officers do not answer to the people. They answer to institutions. A common law sheriff answers to the people because they are the source of his authority.

A community with a strong sheriff becomes resilient. They no longer fear institutions. They no longer rely on statutory courts. They no longer submit to assumed authority. They know their rights. They stand in honour. They resolve disputes through natural law. Enforcement becomes rare because peace becomes common. Peace becomes common because honour becomes the foundation of daily life.

LIMITATIONS OF COMMON LAW COURTS

Common law courts are powerful because they return authority to the people. They restore natural justice. They prioritise honour, consent, and truth. They free the living from statutory assumptions. Yet even with this strength, common law courts have limitations. These limitations do not weaken natural law. They remind the people of their responsibility. They ensure that authority does not become distorted. They protect the purity of the process. Understanding these limitations makes a common law court stronger and prevents misuse.

The first limitation is natural law itself. A common law court cannot act outside natural law. It cannot pursue revenge. It cannot create punishment for the sake of control. It cannot impose obligations without harm, loss, or fraud. Statutory systems create endless offences, penalties, and regulations. Common law recognises only three violations. When a claim does not involve harm, loss, or fraud, the court has no jurisdiction. This limitation keeps the court honest. It prevents the people from becoming an institution that mirrors the systems they reject.

Another limitation is consent. A common law court only has jurisdiction over those who consent to participate. Consent cannot be forced. The court cannot compel attendance. If a man refuses to stand in the court, the court must respond through honour, not coercion. This limitation can be frustrating for those who want quick resolution. Yet it is essential. Natural law is built on agreement. Without agreement, authority becomes domination. A court that forces compliance ceases to be a common law court. It becomes a statutory imitation.

A community must recognise that they cannot drag someone into a hearing as statutory courts do. They cannot insist that someone participates under threat. The living can only stand in honour voluntarily. This truth ensures purity. It ensures fairness. It ensures that the court does not slide into the very behaviour it seeks to replace. A refusal to participate reflects on the individual, not on the court. The community may view refusal as dishonour. They may withdraw trust from the individual. Yet they must not use force. Force belongs to statute, not natural law.

The third limitation involves enforcement. A common law court does not use force to impose remedy. It relies on honour, conscience, and community support. When someone refuses to honour remedy, the court cannot use physical coercion. This limitation ensures that common law enforcement does not become a mirror of statutory enforcement. It protects the court from becoming an institution of punishment. It keeps the focus on restoration.

If a man refuses to honour the remedy, the sheriff may intervene. He may encourage understanding. He may explain the importance of honour. He may involve the community. Yet he cannot impose punishment. He cannot seize the individual. He cannot act with aggression. His power is moral, not physical. This makes common law enforcement stronger in the long term because it relies on internal transformation rather than external pressure. Yet it limits immediate results. A community must understand that natural law works through unity, not force.

Another limitation is scale. A common law court functions best within a community where people know each other. Familiarity builds trust. Trust strengthens authority. In small communities, honour has weight. Reputation is visible. Intent is clearer. When a court operates in a large, disconnected group, these elements weaken. People may not know each other's character. Witnesses may be strangers. Jurors may lack familiarity with the dispute. The effectiveness of natural justice becomes harder to maintain.

A common law court can still function in larger groups, but it must work harder to preserve fairness. The foreman must ensure clarity. The sheriff must ensure peace. The assembly must remain focused on truth rather than emotion. The jury must act with greater care. Large gatherings can bring more confusion. They can bring more noise. They can bring more bias. This limitation does not weaken natural law. It challenges the people to rise to the level required for justice.

A further limitation comes from external interference. Institutions may attempt to disrupt common law courts. They may send representatives. They may claim authority. They may assert statutory jurisdiction. They may threaten proceedings. A common law court must be prepared for such interference. The sheriff must stand firmly. The assembly must remain calm. The people must continue the process. Yet they must not engage in conflict. Conflict weakens natural law. It gives institutions an excuse to escalate.

External interference exposes another limitation. A common law court has no recognised force within statutory systems. Institutions will not acknowledge common law decisions. They will not enforce common law remedy. They will not accept common law jurisdiction. This doesn't make the court invalid. It simply means the court must stand on its own authority. Natural law does not need recognition to exist. Yet the community must accept that statutory systems will not support their decisions. This limitation requires the people to rely on unity rather than external confirmation.

Another limitation comes from misunderstanding. Many people speak of common law without understanding its principles. They repeat phrases. They imitate language. They attempt to use common law tools without honour. They treat common law as a weapon rather than a responsibility. This behaviour weakens the legitimacy of the court. It gives institutions an excuse to dismiss the entire system. A common law court must be built on deep understanding, not superficial claims.

Misunderstanding also arises when people mix statutory concepts with natural law. They attempt to use statutory paperwork in a common law context. They attempt to apply legal arguments from commercial courts. They confuse remedy with penalty. They confuse representation with standing. These confusions can damage a court's legitimacy. A common law court must remain pure. It must rely only on natural principles. It must avoid mixing systems. Mixing systems creates contradiction.

A further limitation is human nature. People carry biases. They carry fears. They carry misunderstandings. A jury must rise above these, yet not every juror will succeed easily. A foreman must guide the process, yet he may make errors. A sheriff must act without ego, yet ego may try to influence him. Common law courts rely on honour. Honour requires discipline. Honour requires humility. Honour requires clarity. These qualities must be cultivated. They do not appear automatically.

Because of this limitation, a community must ensure that participants understand natural law fully. They must be taught. They must be guided. They must be supported. Knowledge strengthens honour. Ignorance weakens it. A court built on ignorance cannot stand. A court built on understanding becomes unshakable. The community must invest time in preparation before forming their court.

A limitation also exists in the area of evidence. Common law courts accept all evidence that reflects truth. This openness is a strength. Yet it also becomes a challenge. People may misinterpret evidence. They may misunderstand testimony. They may give too much weight to opinion. They may confuse emotion with fact. This requires careful guidance. The foreman must remind the assembly to prioritise truth. The jury must weigh evidence carefully. The community must listen with clarity. Natural law reveals truth through conscience, but conscience must be clear.

A final limitation is time. Natural law takes time. It requires listening. It requires understanding. It requires dialogue. It requires deliberation. Statutory courts hurry because they rely on rules, not truth. Common law courts move slowly because they value accuracy. This can be difficult for a community that wants immediate resolution. Yet patience is essential. Justice requires time. Peace requires time. Understanding requires time. A rushed hearing weakens the court. A patient hearing strengthens it.

These limitations do not weaken the authority of common law. They strengthen it. They protect it from becoming corrupted. They remind the community that natural law is not a shortcut. It is a way of life. It demands honour. It demands responsibility. It demands clarity. A common law court that respects its limitations becomes a powerful force of justice.

A common law court gains legitimacy from honour, truth, consent, and clarity. These elements must be protected. When they weaken, the court weakens. When they disappear, the process collapses into confusion or becomes vulnerable to misuse. Understanding the limitations of common law courts allows the community to protect these foundations. It prevents the court from drifting toward the very systems it seeks to replace. Limitations are not weaknesses. They are safeguards.

One limitation comes from the potential misuse of natural law by individuals who act without understanding. Common law is simple, but simplicity requires discipline. When someone uses common law language for personal gain, they harm the entire movement. A man who tries to avoid responsibility by misusing natural law undermines honour. A woman who attempts to avoid remedy by claiming sovereign status without sincerity threatens the legitimacy of the court. People who use natural law as a shield against accountability damage the process. They turn a system meant to restore balance into a tool for evasion. A common law court must guard against this.

The assembly must recognise dishonour. A claim brought in bad faith must be rejected. A man who uses natural law language to deceive must be challenged. A woman who attempts to manipulate the court must be corrected. A community must maintain standards. When the people allow misuse, the court loses authority. When the people refuse to allow misuse, the court becomes stronger. Honour must guide every participant.

Another limitation arises when people bring statutory expectations into a common law process. Many individuals have lived their entire lives under statutory systems. They have been conditioned to expect procedures, penalties, and rigid structures. When they enter a common law court, they may carry these expectations with them. They may expect the court to follow statutory order. They may expect written codes. They may expect complex forms. They may expect strict timelines. These expectations can create confusion.

A common law court must remain vigilant. It must not adopt statutory habits. It must not mimic statutory structures. It must not rely on statutory documentation. These habits corrupt natural law. They turn the court into a hybrid system that lacks clarity. The people must consistently remind themselves that common law is grounded in truth, not in documentation. It thrives through direct communication, not through corporate forms. It gains authority through the living, not through written codes.

A further limitation is the risk of excessive emotion. Natural law requires clarity of conscience. Conscience becomes clouded when emotion takes control. Anger can distort judgment. Fear can silence truth. Sympathy can override fairness. A common law court must recognise these risks. The foreman must guide the process carefully. The sheriff must maintain peace. The jury must remain focused. The assembly must uphold honour. Emotional outbursts may arise because disputes often carry personal weight. Yet these emotions must not control the hearing. Justice requires steady minds.

Another factor that limits the effectiveness of a common law court is the absence of preparation. A community cannot form a court suddenly without understanding natural law. Members must study the principles deeply. They must understand the role of conscience. They must understand the separation between the living and the legal fiction. They must understand consent. They must understand jurisdiction. Without this preparation, the court risks confusion. Confusion attracts interference. Confusion creates division. Confusion weakens authority.

Education becomes essential. The sheriff must guide the people. Experienced members of the assembly must teach newcomers. Jury members must understand their responsibilities. Witnesses must understand the importance of truth. The foreman must understand how to maintain order. When the people prepare, the court becomes strong. When the people neglect preparation, the court becomes vulnerable.

Another limitation emerges when a common law court attempts to extend its authority beyond its own community. Natural law can be universal, but authority is local. A court created by one community cannot impose decisions on another community without consent. Each community must stand in its own authority. Each group must form its own assembly. Each gathering must rely on its own consent. Attempting to impose authority across communities creates confusion. It creates imbalance. It violates natural principles. A community must respect the sovereignty of others.

A limitation also exists regarding resources. A common law court relies entirely on the effort of the people. There are no institutions providing funding. There are no corporate offices organising schedules. There are no salaried officers facilitating the process. Everything depends on voluntary action. This creates strength because it ensures independence. Yet it also creates challenges. People must dedicate time. They must dedicate attention. They must dedicate energy. Without this dedication, the process slows. Delays may occur. Disputes may linger.

This lack of institutional support means a common law court must remain flexible. Hearings may require adjustment. Remedial actions may require coordination. Deputies may need to step in when the sheriff is unavailable. The community must accept these limitations and work within them. Natural law does not promise convenience. It promises fairness. Fairness requires effort.

Another limitation comes from public perception. Many people have been taught to trust statutory systems and fear anything outside them. They have been conditioned to believe that justice comes from courts with robes, flags, and architectural formality. They struggle to recognise justice expressed by ordinary men and women. This conditioning creates hesitation. Individuals may doubt their own authority. They may fear participating. They may question the legitimacy of the process because it does not resemble statutory courts.

A common law court must address this limitation through transparency and education. The people must demonstrate that justice exists in their actions. They must show that fairness does not require buildings or uniforms. They must show that truth arises from conscience, not from formality. The court becomes stronger when it is visible. When people witness the hearing, they see the legitimacy of natural justice. Over time perception changes.

Some limitations arise because institutions may attempt to challenge or undermine the court. They may accuse the people of acting unlawfully. They may attempt to intimidate participants. They may attempt to disrupt gatherings. They may attempt to discredit the sheriff. These attempts expose the insecurity of statutory systems. When institutions see people reclaiming authority, they feel threatened. Their interference reveals their fear.

The sheriff must anticipate such interference. He must remain calm. He must stand in honour. He must remind the people that institutions cannot override natural law. Yet the community must recognise that interference may delay proceedings. It may cause stress. It may disrupt communication. This limitation challenges the people to remain united. Division weakens the court. Unity strengthens it.

Another limitation is human imperfection. People make mistakes. They mishear testimony. They misunderstand evidence. They misjudge character. These imperfections exist in statutory courts as well. Yet statutory courts hide mistakes behind paperwork and procedure. A common law court exposes everything openly. This openness allows the community to correct mistakes. Yet it also exposes flaws in judgment. A community must accept these flaws. They must address them honestly. They must allow correction. They must treat mistakes as opportunities to improve understanding rather than excuses for blame.

A limitation also exists in the enforcement of remedy when individuals reject honour completely. Some people refuse to take responsibility for harm. They refuse to engage with the process. They refuse to recognise the authority of the community. In statutory courts such refusal triggers punishment. In common law courts refusal creates a challenge. The community must decide how to respond. They may withdraw trust. They may refuse association. They may inform others of the dishonour. Social consequences may follow. These consequences are peaceful yet meaningful. They protect the community from further harm.

A final limitation is endurance. Natural law requires commitment. Communities must sustain their court. They must continue to resolve disputes. They must continue to hold hearings. They must continue to support the sheriff. They must continue to educate themselves. This endurance cannot be maintained by a small group alone. It requires widespread participation. When the community grows tired, the court weakens. When the people remain engaged, the court thrives.

These limitations do not diminish the value of common law courts. They remind the people of their role as guardians of natural justice. They show that natural law is not a passive concept. It is a living responsibility. It demands constant attention. It demands clarity. It demands honour. A community that understands these limitations becomes capable of maintaining justice without institutions. They reclaim authority not through force, but through truth.

BUILDING A COMMUNITY COURT SYSTEM

A community court system begins long before the first hearing. It begins when the people recognise that they hold natural authority. It begins when they understand that justice does not come from institutions but from the living. It begins when they decide to take responsibility for their own peace. A common law court is not created in a moment. It is grown. It develops through shared understanding, mutual trust, and collective commitment. The people build it by standing together in honour.

The first step in building a community court system is awakening the people to their own authority. Most individuals have been conditioned to believe that authority comes from the state. They believe courts must have elaborate buildings. They believe justice requires robes and titles. They believe they must depend on institutions for peace. These beliefs weaken natural authority. The people must recognise that justice begins with them. It begins with their ability to listen, to speak truthfully, and to resolve disputes peacefully. This awakening shifts the balance of power.

Once the people recognise their authority, they must form a foundation of understanding. A community cannot operate a court if its members are unclear about natural law. They must learn the principles of harm, loss, and fraud. They must understand consent. They must understand jurisdiction. They must understand the separation between the living and the legal fiction. These concepts cannot be skimmed. They must be absorbed. Understanding strengthens unity. Confusion weakens it.

The sheriff plays an early role in this foundational stage. Even before he is elected, the people look to someone who speaks clearly, someone who explains natural law with sincerity, someone who guides without dominating. This guidance creates momentum. The community begins to see itself as capable of handling disputes without relying on institutions. They begin to discuss common law openly. They begin to recognise when harm occurs. They begin to understand that they have the right, and the responsibility, to repair that harm.

The next step is creating a structure for education. A community that intends to stand under natural law must ensure its members understand the responsibilities involved. This may be done through gatherings where people discuss natural law. It may be done through small groups that study cases. It may be done through open discussions about previous disputes. The purpose is not to create complexity. The purpose is to create clarity. When the people learn together, they build trust. This trust becomes the backbone of the court.

The community must then establish its assembly. The assembly is not an organisation. It is not a registered body. It is simply the gathering of the living. Anyone who consents to participate becomes part of the assembly. The assembly decides when a court is needed. It listens to claims. It supports the sheriff. It oversees the foreman. It provides the environment in which truth can be expressed. The assembly is the heart of the court system. Without it, the process cannot function. With it, the community becomes powerful.

Once the assembly is established, the community must choose how it will select jurors. Jurors must be impartial. They must understand natural law. They must have a strong sense of honour. They must be willing to listen carefully and speak truthfully. The community may decide that jurors are chosen randomly from those who attend. They may decide to rotate jurors regularly. They may decide to select jurors based on experience or temperament. There is no fixed model. Natural law allows flexibility. What matters is fairness. A biased jury weakens the court. A sincere jury strengthens it.

The foreman must also be chosen. The foreman is not a leader. He is a guide. He ensures that the hearing remains orderly. He ensures that both parties are heard. He ensures that the jury has the information it needs. He does not give opinions. He does not dominate discussion. He does not impose authority. The foreman must be someone who understands natural law deeply. He must be calm. He must be patient. He must speak clearly. His presence sets the tone for the entire process.

Once these roles are understood, the community must choose its sheriff. The sheriff will protect the court. He will enforce remedy peacefully. He will stand against unlawful interference. His authority comes only from the people. The election process strengthens the community. It forces people to consider honour. It forces them to recognise who among them they trust. It forces them to reflect on the qualities required to protect natural law. Once elected, the sheriff becomes the stabilising force of the court.

With the assembly, jury structure, foreman, and sheriff in place, the community can begin formalising its court system. This does not mean creating complex rules. It means agreeing on simple guidelines. These guidelines may include how notice is delivered, how hearings are scheduled, how witnesses are invited, how evidence is presented, and how records are kept. These guidelines are not statutes. They are not binding codes. They are agreements rooted in natural principles. They exist to maintain fairness and clarity.

The court must also establish a clear method for keeping records. Records are important because they preserve truth. They show how the court reached its decisions. They show that the community acted in honour. They show that remedy was agreed fairly. These records may be kept by a scribe chosen for their ability to write clearly. A scribe holds no authority. Their role is to document events. These records can be used to resolve misunderstandings. They can protect the court from outside challenges. They demonstrate that the community acted lawfully.

The community must also prepare for disputes. Disputes are inevitable. People misunderstand each other. Harm occurs. Loss is created. Fraud appears. A court system does not prevent disputes. It provides a method for handling them honourably. The community must agree that all disputes involving harm, loss, or fraud may be brought before the court. They must agree that disputes without harm do not belong in the court. They must agree that remedy will always be the goal. These shared expectations make the court functional.

To build a court system, the community must create a culture of honour. Honour is more powerful than any written law. It influences behaviour. It encourages responsibility. It reduces conflict. When honour becomes a shared value, disputes decrease naturally. A community court does not function well in a group that lacks honour. People must be taught the value of honesty. They must be taught the importance of keeping their word. They must be taught the consequences of dishonour. This cultural shift strengthens the court before it even hears its first case.

The community must also understand that the court system is not separate from daily life. It is part of daily life. It influences how people speak to one another. It influences how they resolve disagreements privately. It influences how they treat each other. When the community embraces natural law, they begin to resolve small disputes without the need for hearings. They apologise more quickly. They communicate more clearly. They act with more sincerity. This is one of the greatest signs that the court system is working. The goal is not to hold many hearings. The goal is to create a community where hearings are rarely needed.

The court system must have a clear process for initiating hearings. A man who experiences harm must notify the assembly. A woman who suffers loss must bring her claim to the people. The assembly decides whether a hearing is needed. The foreman prepares the process. Notice is delivered. The jury is selected. The sheriff ensures peace. These steps must be simple. They must be consistent. They must reflect natural law. Complexity destroys fairness. Simplicity strengthens it.

During this early development, the community must also prepare to defend its court peacefully. Institutions may challenge its legitimacy. Officials may attempt to interfere. Statutory officers may arrive uninvited. The sheriff must stand firmly. The assembly must remain calm. The people must assert their authority without aggression. When the community stands together, institutions hesitate. They recognise they cannot override natural law when the people understand it clearly.

A community court system grows into strength through continued practice. Understanding natural law is important, yet true authority emerges when the people apply what they have learned. Knowledge becomes action. Action becomes experience. Experience becomes confidence. Confidence becomes authority. A community that acts under natural law becomes far stronger than one that merely speaks about it. This phase of development transforms a court system from an idea into a living institution grounded in honour.

To move into this phase the community must begin holding regular gatherings. These gatherings do not need to involve disputes. They are opportunities to discuss natural principles, clarify roles, and reinforce unity. They allow the sheriff to speak with the people. They allow the foreman to offer guidance. They allow the scribe to present examples of past cases. Regular gatherings strengthen collective understanding. They create familiarity. They build habit. Habit is important because natural law must become part of daily life, not an occasional idea.

These meetings also help the community identify potential challenges before they arise. The sheriff may explain situations where institutions attempted to trespass. The assembly may discuss misunderstandings that occurred within the community. Jurors may share experiences from previous hearings. People may raise concerns about unclear guidelines. These discussions refine the court system. They prevent confusion. They reduce the risk of disputes escalating unnecessarily.

Another important step in building a community court system is training. While natural law is simple, the roles within the court require skill. Jurors must learn how to listen carefully. The foreman must learn how to maintain balance. The sheriff must learn how to handle interference. The scribe must learn how to document accurately. The assembly must learn how to remain patient and respectful. Training does not need to resemble formal education. It can occur through practice hearings, demonstrations, and open discussions. What matters is consistency. A court cannot function if its members do not understand their responsibilities.

The community must also create a clear method for resolving disputes privately before they reach the court. Disputes that involve minor misunderstandings should be resolved through open dialogue. The sheriff or a respected member of the assembly may mediate. This mediation prevents small disagreements from becoming larger conflicts. When mediation fails, the matter may be brought before the court. This layered approach protects the court from becoming overloaded. It ensures that only matters involving genuine harm, loss, or fraud come before the jury.

As the community continues to develop its court system, it must refine the process of selecting jurors. Jurors must be chosen fairly. Bias must be minimised. Competence must be considered. Some communities choose jurors by random selection. Others select jurors through nomination within the assembly. Others use rotation so that all members participate over time. There is no universal rule. Natural law allows communities to choose the method that suits them. What matters is sincerity. A biased jury weakens justice. A fair jury strengthens it.

The role of the sheriff must also be strengthened. A sheriff becomes more effective when the community supports him openly. This support may take the form of deputies. Deputies assist in maintaining peace during hearings. They help resolve disputes before they escalate. They walk with the sheriff when institutions attempt to interfere. They represent unity. Deputies must be chosen carefully. They must be trusted by the people. They must understand natural law. They must remain calm under pressure. Their presence strengthens the authority of the sheriff.

The court system must also maintain its records responsibly. Records are the written memory of the community. They show how the court handled past disputes. They demonstrate that the process was honourable. They protect the court from accusations of unfairness. They support future decisions by providing examples. Records must be stored safely. They must be accessible to the people. They must be clear. A community that loses its records loses part of its authority.

As the community gains experience, it must prepare to face increasing scrutiny from statutory institutions. Institutions see community court systems as threats. They are not accustomed to people standing under natural law. They rely on submission. When a community asserts its authority, institutions become uncomfortable. They may attempt to challenge the legitimacy of the court. They may claim jurisdiction. They may question the authority of the sheriff. They may attempt to assert statutory power. A prepared community handles this calmly.

The sheriff must respond to institutional challenges with clarity. He must ask the official to prove jurisdiction. He must require evidence of harm. He must remain non-confrontational. Institutions expect resistance. They do not expect calm. Calm exposes the weakness of statutory claims. The community must remain peaceful. They must stand behind their sheriff. Their unity protects their authority. Institutions struggle to act against a community that knows its rights.

Another aspect of building a community court system is strengthening the culture of remedy. Remedy is the foundation of natural justice. It must be central in every hearing. The people must understand that the goal is not victory. The goal is restoration. When someone suffers harm, the responsible party must repair it. When someone causes loss, they must restore it. When someone commits fraud, they must correct it. Remedy heals the community. Punishment divides it.

The people must recognise that remedy is more important than blame. Blame keeps conflict alive. Remedy ends it. A community that focuses on remedy becomes peaceful. A community that focuses on punishment becomes unstable. Statutory systems operate through punishment because punishment generates control. Natural law operates through remedy because remedy generates harmony. This cultural shift strengthens the court.

To support remedy, the community may create a restorative group. This group helps ensure that remedies are carried out. It may include the sheriff, deputies, and respected members of the assembly. They follow up after hearings. They speak with both parties. They check that the remedy is complete. They ensure fairness. Their involvement prevents disputes from returning. This group embodies the court's commitment to peace.

Another key element in developing the court system is transparency. Transparency ensures trust. The people must be able to witness hearings. They must hear the evidence. They must observe the jury. They must understand the decisions. Nothing should be hidden. Secrecy breeds suspicion. Openness strengthens legitimacy. A transparent court becomes respected. A hidden court becomes weak. Transparency protects natural law from corruption.

As the community court system matures, it must prepare for long term sustainability. Natural law does not require institutions, but it requires commitment. New members must be taught. Young people must learn the principles. Elders must pass on wisdom. Roles must be rotated. No one can hold authority indefinitely. A sheriff may step down and a new one may be elected. A foreman may train a successor. Jurors must change over time. This rotation prevents stagnation. It keeps the court alive.

The community must also create a process for handling internal challenges. Disagreements may arise about how the court operates. The assembly must discuss these openly. They must refine guidelines. They must resolve misunderstandings. A court that cannot handle internal conflict cannot handle external disputes. Internal unity is essential. The community must learn to navigate disagreement peacefully. This teaches them how to handle disputes in hearings effectively.

As the people continue to practise natural law, the court system becomes part of their identity. It becomes something they rely on in daily life. When disagreements arise, they speak openly. When harm occurs, they correct it. When confusion appears, they seek clarity. The court becomes a natural extension of community life. It becomes a symbol of sovereignty. It becomes a reminder that authority comes from the living.

Eventually the community will reach a point where natural law becomes second nature. The court will still exist, but it will be called upon less often. This is the greatest sign of success. A court that handles few disputes does so because peace has become the foundation of the community. The people live with honour. They speak truthfully. They act with clarity. They protect each other. This is the purpose of natural law. Not to hold endless hearings, but to create a society where hearings are rarely needed.

THE COURT OF THE LIVING

A common law court is the purest expression of human authority. It is not a system created by governments. It is not a structure imposed by institutions. It is not a ritual owned by courts or councils. It is the natural right of every living soul. It exists wherever men and women stand together in honour. It rises whenever a community refuses to surrender truth to the demands of statute. It thrives when people recognise that justice belongs to the living.

Throughout this book the principles behind common law authority have become clear. Natural law does not depend on paperwork. It does not depend on buildings. It does not depend on titles. It does not depend on written codes. It depends on honour. Honour is the foundation that holds every community together. Without honour there is no peace. Without honour there is no justice. Without honour there is no authority. When honour becomes the guiding force, law becomes simple. It becomes accessible. It becomes alive.

A community that stands in natural authority becomes stronger than any institution. Institutions rely on assumptions. They rely on silence. They rely on fear. They rely on the belief that the people do not know their rights. Natural law strips away these assumptions. It shows the people that they outrank statutory roles. It shows them that consent creates all lawful authority. It shows them that no government can impose control on the living without agreement. Once the people understand this, the balance shifts. Fear disappears. Clarity returns. Authority returns to its rightful place.

A common law court is a reminder that justice does not belong to officials. It belongs to the community. It is created by the people. It is applied by the people. It is enforced by the people. It is protected by the people. This truth is powerful because it cannot be taken away. It cannot be revoked by statute. It cannot be overridden by regulation. It cannot be diluted by commercial courts. Natural authority exists because the living exist.

When a community forms its court, it steps into its rightful position. It reclaims what has always belonged to the people. It rejects the idea that justice must be delegated to institutions. It refuses to act as the legal fiction. It refuses to accept assumed jurisdiction. It declares that the living stand under natural law. This declaration is not rebellion. It is restoration. It restores balance. It restores dignity. It restores peace. It returns law to the hands of those who live under it.

Through their court the people learn to listen again. They learn to speak truth. They learn to recognise deception. They learn to resolve disputes without force. They learn to repair harm rather than escalate it. They learn to protect each other. These lessons strengthen every aspect of community life. They influence how people treat each other outside the court. They influence how families resolve conflict. They influence how neighbours interact. They influence how the community responds to external pressure.

A common law sheriff stands as the guardian of this authority. His role is not to dominate. His role is not to punish. His role is not to enforce statute. His role is to protect peace. His authority flows from the people. His duty is to uphold natural law. When institutions attempt to trespass, he stands in the way. When disputes arise, he guides the remedy. When fear attempts to take hold, he brings clarity. His presence strengthens unity. His integrity strengthens trust. His honour strengthens law.

The common law court teaches the people that justice is not a distant concept. It is not an abstract theory. It is not something that happens behind closed doors. It lives in every interaction. It lives in every decision. It lives in every gathering. It lives in the willingness of the people to hold themselves accountable. When the people embrace this responsibility, justice becomes part of daily life. Disputes decrease. Unity increases. Peace becomes stable.

The limitations of common law courts are not weaknesses. They are safeguards. They prevent corruption. They prevent misuse. They prevent the court from becoming a mirror of statutory systems. They remind the people that they must act with integrity. They remind them that they cannot force participation. They remind them that they must rely on honour rather than coercion. These limitations protect the purity of natural law. They preserve the value of the court.

Building a community court system is a long process. It requires learning. It requires humility. It requires patience. It requires unity. Yet once built, it becomes a source of strength. It becomes a place where truth is spoken without fear. It becomes a place where remedy replaces punishment. It becomes a place where people rediscover their authority. It becomes a place where the living stand in dignity.

A community that understands natural law cannot be controlled in the same way as those who depend on statutory systems. They recognise their rights. They understand consent. They understand jurisdiction. They understand the difference between lawful authority and assumed power. They see through deception. They stand calmly in truth. This calmness is more powerful than any statute. It cannot be overcome by intimidation. It cannot be shaken by threats. It cannot be silenced by authority that lacks natural foundation.

The common law court is not a tool for rebellion. It is a tool for restoration. It restores the natural balance between the people and the systems around them. It restores the principle that authority must serve the living. It restores the understanding that justice is a shared responsibility. It restores peace through remedy. It restores respect through honour. It restores unity through truth.

When a community embraces this truth, it changes. People walk with more confidence. They speak with more clarity. They treat each other with more respect. They recognise their own value and the value of others. They reject fear. They reject confusion. They reject the idea that external institutions hold superior authority. They know that natural law comes from within. They know that their court expresses their sovereignty. They know that justice belongs to them.

This book has guided the people toward that understanding. It has shown them how to form their court. It has shown them how to choose their sheriff. It has shown them how to run hearings. It has shown them how to enforce remedy peacefully. It has shown them how to build a system that reflects the truth of the living. Now the responsibility rests with the community. They must decide whether they will stand in honour. They must decide whether they will reclaim their authority. They must decide whether they will build their court.

Natural law is waiting. It waits for the living to remember who they are. It waits for the people to recognise their power. It waits for the community to stand together. When they do, justice returns to its rightful place. Peace becomes possible. Honour becomes the foundation. Truth becomes the guide. The court of the living rises.

Don't miss out!

Visit the website below and you can sign up to receive emails whenever Roger Davies publishes a new book. There's no charge and no obligation.

https://books2read.com/r/B-A-HHGNE-GAGKI

BOOKS 2 READ

Connecting independent readers to independent writers.

Did you love *Common Law Courts and Sheriffs: Restoring the Authority of the People*? Then you should read *I Do Not Consent: A Sovereign Guide to Standing in Your Own Authority*[1] by Roger Davies!

[2]

You were born free. You were not born as a record, a number, a role, or a function. You were born as the living man or the living woman. The world teaches you to forget this. Governments, councils, banks, and officials behave as though your silence is agreement. They behave as though your signature is automatic. They behave as though your consent exists even when you never gave it. Many people feel this pressure but do not have the words to express it. They know something is wrong. They know the system uses assumption. They know authority is taken through habit, not agreement.

This book speaks to those people. It speaks to those who already know they are sovereign. It speaks to those who refuse to live under silent contracts. It speaks to those who feel the artificial world pressing against them and want to stand in their own authority without fear.

---

1. https://books2read.com/u/mVzdv6

2. https://books2read.com/u/mVzdv6

I Do Not Consent is a clear and strong guide for the living being who wants to understand how modern systems claim power and how to withdraw consent calmly. It shows how institutions rely on presumption, confusion, roles, and unexamined behaviour. It explains how most authority is offered, not imposed. It shows how consent is taken through silence and how silence can be replaced with calm truth.

You will learn the difference between the living being, the recorded identity, and the assumed identity. You will see how institutions use these layers to bind the living without open agreement. You will learn how to separate yourself from roles that were never chosen. You will learn how to remove presumption, how to refuse unwanted authority, how to stand as the living, and how to protect your own inner freedom.

This book does not teach conflict. It teaches clarity. It teaches calm presence. It teaches simple actions that prevent silent contracts. It teaches how to speak from the living and how to question claims that rely on pressure instead of proof. It shows how fear is used to control behaviour and how to replace that fear with steady awareness.

Every idea in this work is written for people who already feel the pull toward sovereignty. It strengthens that pull. It clarifies it. It supports it. It gives structure to what many already sense within themselves. It is for those who know they do not belong to any system. It is for those who choose their own path. It is for those who say the words I do not consent and mean them.

If you want to understand how the system operates without attacking it, this book shows you.If you want to stand as the living without confusion, this book guides you.If you want to speak truth without fear, this book strengthens you.If you want to reclaim your own authority, this book supports you.

You do not need permission to be sovereign.You do not need approval to stand as the living.You do not need fear to guide your choices.

Your authority begins with you.Your consent belongs to you.Your path belongs to you.

I Do Not Consent is written for those who already know this and want to live it with clarity and strength.

Also by Roger Davies

Adventures in Sovereignty: Growing Up Free
The Secret of the Hidden Name

Sovereign Action
Cease the Decree: Ending Contracts in Peace
I Do Not Consent: A Sovereign Guide to Standing in Your Own Authority
Council Tax Nullity: How to Challenge Local Tax Demands through Honour and Law
I Require Proof: A Sovereign Guide to Breaking Presumption and Exposing False Authority
The Private Record: How to Build Lawful Evidence of Truth and Standing
I Stand Recorded: A Sovereign Guide to Notice, Response and Written Authority

Sovereign Foundations: Liberty, Rights, Consent
The Constitution of One: How the Bill of Rights Protects the Sovereign Man & Woman
From Subjects to Sovereigns: Reclaiming the Spirit of 1776
Liberty by Consent: Reclaiming Freedom Through the Law of Consent

Standalone

The Commonwealth Corporation: How Australia Was Turned Into a Business
The Legal Fiction: The Greatest Trick Ever Played on Humanity
The Sovereign Path: Living Free Beyond the System
Common Law: The True Law of the Living
Freedom by Rebuttal: How to Say No and Stand Free
The Magna Carta: Why It Is Important to Sovereign Men and Women
The Trust Game: Hidden Estates and the Cestui Que Vie Act
Freedom by Notice: Winning with Paperwork
The Hidden Contracts: How Governments Enslave the People
The Law of the Living: Admiralty Shadows and the Path to Sovereignty
Standing as a Living Man or Woman in Canada: Reclaiming Freedom Beyond Statutes and Policy
Sovereign Stories for Children: 14 Parables of Freedom, Truth, and Honour
The Definitive Sovereign Handbook: Do No Harm, Cause No Loss, Commit No Fraud
Lose the Fear: Be Sovereign and Free
Sovereign 2026: Losing the Fear
When Council Tax Fear Takes Over: How to steady your mind and regain your internal peace
The Truth Movement: Breaking Presumption, Reclaiming Freedom, Living as Sovereign
Common Law Courts and Sheriffs: Restoring the Authority of the People

About the Author

Roger Davies researches the crossroads of commerce, policy, and personal sovereignty. He writes for readers who sense there is more to the story, who are ready to replace fear with honour and paperwork with plain truth. When not writing, he helps men and women organise their records, challenge unfounded claims, and build communities grounded in mutual aid and responsibility.

www.ingramcontent.com/pod-product-compliance
Lightning Source LLC
LaVergne TN
LVHW090416210926
848480LV00002B/584
* 9 7 9 8 2 3 1 3 7 9 2 7 9 *